A Walk in the Parks

The definitive guidebook to monuments in Charleston's major downtown parks — including White Point Garden, Marion Square, Waterfront Park and Washington Square.

By John R. Young
Registered Charleston Tour Guide

A Walk in the Parks

The definitive guidebook to monuments in Charleston's major downtown parks — including White Point Garden, Marion Square, Waterfront Park and Washington Square.

By John R. Young
Registered Charleston Tour Guide

EVENING
POST
PUBLISHING
COMPANY
Charleston
South Carolina

EVENINGPOSTBOOKS
Our Accent is Southern!
www.EveningPostBooks.com

Published by
Evening Post Books
Charleston, South Carolina
www.EveningPostBooks.com

Editors: John M. Burbage, Jason Lesley
Design and maps: Gill Guerry
Photographers: Tatjana Mihailovic, Katharine Young,
Jason Lesley

First printing 2010
Printed in the United States of America

A CIP catalog record for this book has been applied
for from the Library of Congress.

ISBN: 978-0-9825154-4-0

Index

Introduction

At the dedication of Waterfront Park in 1990, Charleston Mayor Joseph P. Riley Jr. said, "The lasting mark of a civilization is a city, and a city cannot have too many parks. They soften the hard edges of urban life, invigorate us, and give us peace and repose."

I agree wholeheartedly. Green space is a precious commodity and Charlestonians are very, very lucky. The city has 90 parks and 1,200 acres of open space.

The city's recognition of the importance of these public places goes back to the 19th century. The tradition of erecting monuments in these beautiful spaces is almost as long. However, at times, these public displays of recognition and remembrance seem to be at cross-

Children frolic in the fountain at Waterfront Park.

purposes to the primary reasons people visit parks. If we go to seek peace, quiet and relaxation, why are our parks filled with war memorials, weapons and statues of dead generals, politicians and other men? The simple answer is: Some organization decided the monuments were important.

Although Charleston's monuments do offer glimpses into the city and state history and values, unfortunately, in most cases, a full understanding is almost impossible.

As an experienced Charleston tour guide, I take great pride in sharing the history and the values. The parks are tailor-made for that purpose. However, the problem has been that Charleston had no single comprehensive source for accessing this material. Well, folks, you hold in your hands a Rosetta stone for exploring the four major downtown parks — White Point Garden, Marion Square, Waterfront Park and Washington Square.

I have been as comprehensive as possible. Although much of the information stands alone and can be appreciated independently of the monuments, this book is specifically designed as a guide to enhance your on-site experience.

I have scrupulously inspected the monuments for details that have been overlooked in earlier descriptions. In doing so, I have found both errors of omission and commission, as well as a tendency to accept earlier published sources without question.

A number of small items:

• When I give the dimensions of monuments, I take a practical tack. If easily measurable, I measure them. In cases where this is impractical, I cite the source of the measurements. Or, as a last resort, I make an educated guess. To be clear, my daredevil days are behind me. I most certainly did not shimmy up the Washington Light Infantry Monument, and I did not scale the Calhoun Monument. For any dimensions I did not personally take, I use the following sort of explanation: The Hampton Obelisk is described as 25 feet in height (May 28, 1912 — The News and Courier).

• I make no attempt to convert historical dollar or pound values. Anytime a figure is given, it's from the respective time period.

• During the city's history, it has been called Charles Towne, then Charlestown and eventually Charleston. I have chosen these somewhat arbitrary parameters: Charles Towne (1670-1719) — Proprietary Colony; Charlestown (1720-1782) — Royal Colony and Revolutionary War; and Charleston (1783-present) — City Incorporation.

• Although there are many references to the "Civil War" in this book, this is the only time you will see the term used in my writing. I have adopted the Southern attitude to our four-year-long national struggle: "Sir, there was nothing civil about that war!" Note the variety of expressions and, in many cases, the passion still associated with "The War."

A landscaped sidewalk in Marion Square.

I am not a native of Charleston. I have lived in the area a mere 16 years. I lived in Vermont for my first 43. Although I may have an outsider's perceptions and prejudices, I have come to love the area and its history, warts and all. I hope my passion comes through in this effort. I also hope you enjoy the end product as much as I enjoyed the process of compiling it. Although I view this guide as a work in progress and intend to update it over the years as new information becomes available, I believe it offers a one-stop source to enhance your enjoyment of some of Charleston's great treasures.

A final personal note: A more serious writer would stick to presenting the facts associated with the parks and their features. However, I do not place myself among that illustrious group. For better or worse, you will find this book peppered with my opinions, observations, trivia and what passes for humor.

Have fun!

White Point Garden

M ajestic live oaks dominate the city's best-known park, providing much-needed shade for visitors and Charlestonians alike
during long, hot, humid summers.

The Location

White Point Garden is a 6.54-acre park at the southern tip of the
Charleston peninsula and between East Battery Street, South Battery
Street, King Street and Murray Boulevard.

The History

White Point Garden is the park's official name but sometimes it is called White Point "Gardens." These names refer to the white sand and piles of bleached oyster shells the original settlers spied at the tip of the Charleston peninsula. For many years, the entire area was referred to as White Point or Oyster Point, but eventually, the term was applied only to the southernmost tip. The park is also called Battery Park, or for most Charlestonians, simply The Battery. These names refer to the numerous batteries — emplacements of heavy guns or fortifications equipped with such guns — that helped defend the city over the years.

By the early 1700s there were some fortifications and cannon on the site. More substantial construction began in 1737 when Battery Broughton was built where Church Street meets South Battery Street today. Construction continued through the 1740s, but the 1752 hurricane demolished most of the town's fortifications.

In 1755, in anticipation of war with France, military engineer William De Brahm oversaw construction of some additional defenses, including earthworks to connect the Broughton fortifications to those at the Granville Bastion, where the Missroon House (40 East Bay Street) is today. A portion of the brick fortifications still exists there.

During the American Revolution, more defenses were constructed in the area. After the Revolution and into the 19th century, the filling of marshland and mudflats that would become park grounds was coincidental to the creation of a seawall along most of modern-day East Battery Street and a portion of East Bay Street.

In 1837, Mayor Henry Laurens Pinckney hired noted New York architect Charles F. Reichardt to draw up plans to turn the area surrounding White Point into a "public pleasure park." In the late 1830s and 1840s, the city purchased land between South Battery and the Ashley River. Between 1848 and 1852, additional acquisitions were made as the seawall was extended west to the end of King Street. This area was subsequently filled.

During the course of the War of Northern Aggression, two earthwork forts — Battery Ramsay and the King Street Battery — were built in the park.

After the 1886 earthquake, White Point and all the other city parks became tent cities, affording temporary shelter for some of Charleston's 40,000 newly homeless, including both rich and poor, black and white.

In 1896, John Charles Olmsted (1852-1920), nephew and adopted son of famed landscape architect Frederick Law Olmsted, surveyed the area and made a series of recommendations to the city, including a park design. Although his design was not implemented, another was used to create the boulevard. Between 1909 and 1911, the city filled 47 more acres of marsh and mudflats along the Ashley River.

By 1922 the completion of a road at the edge of the filled land,

White Point Garden

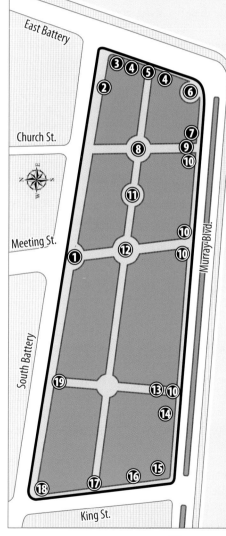

East Battery

Church St.

Meeting St.

South Battery

Murray Blvd.

King St.

Key for map and descriptions that follow

1. Torpedo Boat Monument
2. Pirate Marker
3. Dahlgren Gun
4. Confederate Columbiads
5. William Moultrie Statue
6. Defenders of Fort Sumter
7. Brooke Rifle
8. Defenders of Fort Moultrie
9. Fake Four-Pounder
10. Thirteen-Inch Mortars
11. Simms Memorial
12. Williams Music Pavilion
13. Little Dancer
14. Amberjack Memorial
15. Hobson Monument
16. WW I Howitzer
17. French Cannon
18. USS Maine Capstan
19. Rapid-Fire Gun

the Boulevard (later named Murray Boulevard), and the extension of East Battery Street to join the two, created the park's current configuration.

The park features two bench styles. The iron-and-wood Charleston Battery Benches are at the edges of the park, facing outward, while the concrete-and-wood Colonial Lake Benches are placed deep within the park. Perhaps these two styles represent, respectively, the extrovert and the introvert of outdoor public furniture.

In 2008 plans for a major rehabilitation of White Point Garden were announced. Although the basic character of the park was to remain unchanged, improvements included resetting or replacing curbing, brick edging, oyster shell paths, retaining walls and sidewalks. Lighting and irrigation would be improved, benches added, and other areas re-sodded and landscaped. Wherever possible, existing materials would be preserved. The pace of rehabilitation depended on available funding.

1. Torpedo Boat Monument

One's eye is immediately drawn to the twin waterspouts. Referred to as dolphins, they actually look more like aquatic gargoyles. The distraction is unfortunate because the monument honors some of the Confederacy's bravest.

The Details

The drinking fountain's northern face has the names of the two organizations responsible for the monument's installation, and the month and year of dedication. The lettering is raised and polished. There are also two indentations, possibly cut as cup holders.

The southern face has the dedication. Below the dedication is a listing of *two attacks without loss of life,* one each by the torpedo boats *Torch* and *David* on the Union blockader *New Ironsides.*

In addition, an attempt was made to list those who died serving aboard the *H.L. Hunley,* the Confederate submarine, opening with the statement: *Of More Than Thirty Men Drowned In This Desperate Service The Names Of Only Sixteen Are Known.* Today the names or partial names of all 21 are known.

Not listed are Absolum Williams, John Kelly, Frank Doyle, Nicholas Davis and Michael Cane, all of whom died August 29, 1863, when an accident caused the submarine to submerge prematurely.

On October 15, 1863, an inadvertent dive plowed the subma-rine bow-first into the bottom of the harbor, causing the deaths of Horace Lawson Hunley, Robert Brookbank, Joseph Patterson, Thomas W. Park, Charles McHugh, Henry Beard, John Marshall and Charles L. Sprague. The list is mostly accurate, except Brook-bank's surname is "Brockbank." Although Hunley is described as the submarine's inventor, investor/owner would be more accurate. James R. McClintock, Baxter Watson and William A. Alexander were the inventor/builders.

Of those lost February 17, 1864, in the successful attack on the

Union warship *Housatonic* — Lt. George E. Dixon, C.F. Carlson, Joseph Ridgeway, C. Simkins, F. Collins, James A. Wicks, a man named Miller, and Arnold Becker — four of the names are completely accurate. However, C.F. Carlson is now believed to have been "J.F. Carlsen." Joseph Ridgeway is thought to have been "Joseph Ridgaway." C. Simkins has been corrected to "C. Lumpkin," and F. Collins now has a first name, "Frank."

Viett Marble Works of Charleston designed and installed the work. The Winnsboro Granite Company of Winnsboro, S.C., contributed the stone. The monument is 7 feet tall and stands on an oblong-shaped 16-foot-by-9-foot brick plaza, edged with granite. The memorial has a bit of an unfinished quality, and in several places drill marks are visible.

In the 1970s, the original spouts were removed and replicas were substituted. Parts of two pins, likely from the originals, can still be seen.

Vehicles have struck the monument on several occasions. Drivers coming down Meeting Street don't always realize that straight ahead is not an option. In November 1979 a motorcyclist rammed it and was killed. Another accident in 1993 led to installing sturdier structural bollards, building a new base, re-plumbing the fountain and resetting the monument.

The History

Although often referred to as the Hunley or Submarine Monument, the granite drinking fountain is dedicated to all Confederate sailors who served in the torpedo fleet. The fleet consisted of the hand-cranked *H.L. Hunley*, the originally oar- and later steam-powered *Torch*, and the steam-powered, semi-submersible *David*.

During the War for Southern Liberty, a torpedo was a copper cylinder filled with black powder and armed with fuses. Each of the boats had a long barb-tipped spar. By ramming an enemy warship, the spar and torpedo were attached. Next, the Confederate vessel reversed course, and from a safe distance, the lanyard was pulled and the charge ignited. The Union referred to these boats as "Confederate rams." All of these vessels were employed in an attempt to break the Union blockading fleet's tightening stranglehold on the port of Charleston.

The Dedication

The United Daughters of the Confederacy and the Charleston Memorial Association raised $1,000 through donations. The memorial was dedicated May 8, 1899. However, the four-day Convention of United Confederate Veterans, which attracted 30,000 visitors to the city, overshadowed the low-key ceremonies.

On a personal note: I've wondered about the apparent lack of sensitivity in having a drinking fountain as a memorial to men who drowned. But then again, maybe it's just me.

NEAR THIS SPOT IN THE AUTUMN OF 1718,
STEDE BONNET, NOTORIOUS "GENTLEMAN
PIRATE", AND TWENTY NINE OF HIS MEN,
CAPTURED BY COLONEL WILLIAM RHETT,
MET THEIR JUST DESERTS AFTER A TRIAL
AND CHARGE, FAMOUS IN AMERICAN HISTORY,
BY CHIEF JUSTICE NICHOLAS TROTT,
LATER NINETEEN OF RICHARD WORLEY'S CREW
CAPTURED BY GOVERNOR ROBERT JOHNSON,
WERE ALSO FOUND GUILTY AND HANGED.
ALL WERE BURIED OFF WHITE POINT GARDENS,
IN THE MARSH BEYOND LOW-WATER MARK

2. Pirate Marker

Reading the inscription on the granite monument transports the passerby back to the heady days of the Golden Age of Piracy.

The 18th Century History

If you'd been a pirate in 1718, you would have been wise to steer clear of Charles Towne, and even that might not have saved you. During a week long blockade in May of that year, Blackbeard (Edward Teach) captured nine ships, held wealthy Charlestonians hostage and elicited a ransom from the city. The citizenry demanded revenge. In September, Colonel William Rhett, leading a contingent of militiamen, launched a retaliatory expedition to the Cape Fear River of North Carolina and netted former Barbadian sugarcane planter Stede Bonnet, "The Gentleman Pirate," and 34 of his mates. In November, Proprietary Governor Robert Johnson led another group of militiamen in clearing the harbor of a pirate ship commanded by Richard

Worley, who died in the confrontation.

The 20th Century History

At the July 8, 1941, Historical Commission meeting, Chairman Daniel Ravenel noted the removal of a wooden "pirate marker" at the residence of Mrs. William Watts Ball (14 Water Street) and proposed that the commission place a stone marker, possibly near the corner of Church and Water streets. Eventually, the commission selected a site in White Point Garden.

J. Harold Easterby, commission member and professor of history at the College of Charleston, wrote the monument's text. E.J. McCarthy & Sons Monument Co. was contracted to erect a Light Elberton Blue granite stone with a sand-and-cement foundation. The monument's cost was $150, plus a 25-cents-a-letter inscription charge. It's unclear when the marker was erected. On November 13, 1943, the Charleston Evening Post noted the marker's placement. The next day, the News and Courier reported that a seven-foot granite marker had been erected near East Battery Street (actually closer to South Battery). The article indicated that the words were inscribed directly into the granite to conserve bronze for the war effort.

The Details

The marker commemorates the 1718 captures, trials and executions of Stede Bonnet and 29 of his men, along with 19 members of Richard Worley's crew. The marker reads:

NEAR THIS SPOT IN THE AUTUMN OF 1718, STEDE BONNET, NOTORIOUS "GENTLEMAN PIRATE," AND TWENTY NINE OF HIS MEN, CAPTURED BY COLONEL WILLIAM RHETT, MET THEIR JUST DESERTS AFTER A TRIAL AND CHARGE, FAMOUS IN AMERICAN HISTORY, BY CHIEF JUSTICE NICHOLAS TROTT. LATER NINETEEN OF RICHARD WORLEY'S CREW, CAPTURED BY GOVERNOR ROBERT JOHNSON, WERE ALSO FOUND GUILTY AND HANGED. ALL WERE BURIED OFF WHITE POINT GARDENS, IN THE MARSH BEYOND LOW-WATER MARK.

The inscription oversimplifies the details. There were actually 10 separate trials and three executions. The first of the trials of the 33 members of Bonnet's crew started October 28, 1718; 29 were eventually sentenced to death on November 5 and "danced the hempen jig" three days later.

Bonnet escaped October 25 and was at large until November 5 before being recaptured by Colonel Rhett. Following a two-day trial, he was sentenced on November 12, but was not executed until December 10.

The 19 survivors of Worley's crew were captured on November 5, given a speedy trial and executed within days.

One small point concerns the use of the preposition "beyond" on the marker. The word "at" may have been more appropriate as it would've been impractical to conduct burials beyond low-water mark.

Part of the rationale for the marker's placement in White Point had to do with a special event held there starting in 1936 during the Azalea Festival (1934-1942 and sporadically after that). The mid-April festival drew thousands to the city. One of the highlights, especially for children, was the Pirate Pageant, an elaborate reenactment of Bonnet and his crew's trials, convictions and executions. For several years, Charleston businessman Francis B. Stewart played the role of Bonnet. On the day of the event, he always posted a sign on the front door of his shop that read: "Gone to the Hanging."

3. Dahlgren Gun

This imposing cannon offers no clues to either its value or the desperate and ingenious measures employed to wrest it from Union hands.

In 1862 the 11-inch Dahlgren gun was cast in Boston. It is one of a pair once mounted in the Union warship *Keokuk*. The *Keokuk* was an experimental, twin-turreted ironclad — a steam-powered vessel protected by iron or steel armor plates — with one Dahlgren in each turret.

When nine Union ironclads attacked Fort Sumter on April 7, 1863, the *Keokuk* was so badly riddled that it sank off Morris Island and was abandoned by the Union Navy.

Confederate General P.G.T. Beauregard ordered a salvage attempt. Although it was not going to be easy to recover two 13-foot guns, each weighing 16,000 pounds, the Dahlgrens were desperately needed to shore up the city's defenses. And so, under cover of darkness at

low tide, whenever the weather was calm, Confederate salvors began the slow and dangerous recovery process. The turrets' armor plates were removed, and the iron beams beneath the guns were cut away. Finally, men swam down into the turrets and unbolted the guns from their carriages. All of this was accomplished barely a thousand yards from Union-controlled territory.

When all was in readiness and the tides and weather favorable, an old lightship hulk, modified with shears and tackle to lift the massive guns, was towed to the site by a steamship. Lines were attached and eventually, with effort and luck, one of the guns was hoisted out of the water and conveyed to the city. A few nights later, the second gun was recovered.

The entire operation took two and a half weeks. The guns were then used in the Confederate defense of Charleston. One disappeared after the war and possibly sold for scrap.

The remaining gun was placed in the park in 1899.

4. Confederate Columbiads

Within the park, there are two Model 1861, 10-inch smoothbores — cannon having no grooves or ridges (rifling) on the inner surface of the barrel.

Although not visible, identification marks on the trunnions — the metal projections that allow mounting — indicate that one (to the right of the Moultrie monument) was built by Junius L. Archer's Bellona Foundry, near Richmond, date of manufacture unknown. The other (to the left of the Moultrie monument) was built by J.R. Anderson & Co., commonly known as the Tredegar Foundry, also of Richmond, in 1862.

The guns were moved to the park in 1900.

5. William Moultrie Statue

The statue portrays Colonel William Moultrie staring into the distance, his hat firmly clutched in his right hand, his eyes eagerly searching the horizon for the white sails of the approaching British warships on the eve of the Battle of Sullivan's Island.

The Details

In April 2007, the battleship *Maine*'s capstan was removed from the site. (For details see Maine Capstan — White Point.) In May, the soil was strengthened to accommodate the new base and statue. A concrete pad was laid atop the newly compacted soil.

Christopher Liberatos of Charleston designed the pedestal. E.J. McCarthy & Sons of Charleston did the cutting, sandblasting, carving, lettering and even the setting of the steel-finish pedestal. Richard Crites, McCarthy's owner, described the base as 5½-feet-by-5½-feet and 8-feet-9-inches tall and weighing 44,000 pounds. The pedestal is composed of five stacked pieces of Elberton Gray granite. As each piece was added, bags of ice were placed between the sections so the hoisting straps could be easily removed. When the ice melted, the stone was drilled, pinned and epoxied. Bluestone pavers surround the pedestal's base. The pedestal's East Battery face holds a large inscription — MOULTRIE. The Murray Boulevard face is inscribed with the principal organizations responsible for the project. The South Battery face is inscribed with the names of other organizations that supported the effort. The King Street face includes a brief biography, highlighting Moultrie's military and political careers. Below the biography is the dedication date — June 28, 2007.

The cost of the project was approximately $250,000.

There is a small problem with the base's triglyphs — classical ornamentation involving three bars. They're upside down. They can be seen near the base's top. The E-shaped ornamentation is standing on its head, like a "W," instead of on its feet, like an "M."

Ward Sculptural Arts Foundry of Atlanta cast the 8-foot-tall statue.

The Sculptor

John N. Michel (1943-) is the sculptor. He was born in Atlanta, Ga. He received his MFA in sculpture from the Tyler School of Art in Philadelphia, Pa. He was a professor of fine arts at the College of Charleston (1973-2004). Although his works can be found throughout the country, the greatest number are in the Charleston area, both on public display and in private collections. He has completed numerous bronze and stone "portraits" (busts), including one of Charleston attorney Gedney Howe Jr., which can be seen at the entrance to the Charleston County Judicial Center. The Washington statue in Washington Square is also his work.

The Biography

William Moultrie (1730-1805) was born in Charlestown, the son of John, a Scottish-born physician, and Lucretia Cooper Moultrie. He married Damaris Elizabeth de St. Julien in December 1749. The couple had three children, two surviving to adulthood. In 1779 fol-

lowing his first wife's death, Moultrie married Hannah Motte Lynch, widow of wealthy rice planter and patriot Thomas Lynch Sr. Through Moultrie's first marriage and subsequent land purchases, he acquired a large estate in St. John's Berkeley Parish.

In 1752 Moultrie won election to the Commons House of Assembly, representing his home district. Over the next 40 years, he served in royal, revolutionary and state assemblies.

During the French and Indian War, Moultrie began his military service in the militia campaigns against the Cherokees. By 1774 he attained the rank of colonel. The following year, he became commander of the 2nd South Carolina Regiment of Foot.

Moultrie achieved national fame on June 28, 1776, as commander of the militia that defeated the British fleet at the Battle of Sullivan's Island. [See Defenders of Fort Moultrie — White Point Garden for more details.] Soon after this early American victory, the palmetto-log-and-sand fort was named in his honor. The following September, Moultrie's regiment was made part of the Continental Army and he was promoted to brigadier general.

In February 1779 at the Battle of Port Royal, Moultrie and his men drove the British from the Beaufort area. In May he helped save Charlestown from an attack by a small, mobile force out of

British-held Florida.

The following year, the British Army and Navy returned to Charlestown. On May 12, 1780, Charlestown fell to a British siege. Moultrie was made a prisoner on parole, confined with other Continental officers at Haddrell's Point in modern-day Mount Pleasant. Due to his Loyalist connections (two of his brothers sided with the British), he was asked to change his allegiance. He firmly declined. By February 1782 he was exchanged for Maj. Gen. John Burgoyne. He continued to serve until war's end, achieving the rank of major general.

Moultrie resumed his political career in 1783, serving in the South Carolina General Assembly. A year later, he was elected lieutenant governor, and in February 1785 was elected governor. His legislative and military skills were put to the test in the post-Revolutionary years. He presided over the state as it struggled to re-establish credit, reorganize the militia, create a county court system, improve internal navigation and relocate the capital to the newly created city of Columbia. At the end of his term in 1787, he was elected to the South Carolina Senate. He represented his parish during the ratifying process the following year. The convention was held at the Old Exchange in Charleston, and on May 23, 1788, he was among the majority approving ratification of the U.S. Constitution. He resigned the Senate in 1791 and a year later was again elected governor. In 1792 his reputation was damaged when his half-brother, Andrew, longtime state attorney general, was impeached for financial misconduct. Moultrie also drew fire for his support of the French Revolution.

After his controversial second term, Moultrie returned to private life. He had suffered great financial losses during the Revolution and his fortunes continued to decline afterward. Nonetheless, he was held in high esteem, serving as president of the state Society of the Cincinnati, a fraternal organization composed of former Continental Army officers, from its establishment until his death. In retirement, he published "Memoirs of the American Revolution."

The History

Three attempts to honor General Moultrie with a statue failed, the earliest going back to 1829, another a century later, and most recently in 1975. George L. Brailsford, ninth generation Moultrie descendant, began the fourth effort in 1998 as a family project. Soon, he enlisted three organizations that shared his ambition and passion — the Society of the Cincinnati of the State of South Carolina, the Society of Colonial Wars in the State of South Carolina and the Major General William Moultrie Chapter, South Carolina Society Sons of the American Revolution. In 2000, the Major General William Moultrie Statue Committee was formed and Brig. Gen. Francis (Frank) D. Rogers Jr., USAF (Ret.) was appointed chairman. Brailsford was, in effect, Gen. Rogers' executive officer for the project's duration. Over the course of seven years, the contributions of many other organizations and hundreds of individuals made the fourth time the charm. The goal of all those involved was to promote education and tourism.

The Dedication

On June 28, 2007, the 231st anniversary of the Battle of Sullivan's Island, the statue of Maj. Gen. Moultrie was dedicated. The Palmetto Society, which organizes Carolina Day — the annual celebration of the victory at the Battle of Sullivan's Island — incorporated the dedication ceremony into the day's events. Normally, ceremonies are held around the Defenders of Fort Moultrie Monument.

It was a beautiful day, with temperatures in the mid-80s, low humidity and refreshing breezes. Beneath the shady live-oak canopy, hundreds gathered to honor the commander of the Fort Sullivan militiamen.

Prior to the dedication, the traditional Carolina Day parade marched from Washington Square to White Point. As usual, most of the city's diverse social, patriotic, genealogical, fraternal, military and historical organizations were represented. The organizations are arranged chronologically, according to date of founding. The

St. Andrew's Society (est. 1729) always leads the parade. While the procession made its way down Meeting Street to White Point, the Charleston Community Band, conducted by Commander J. Michael Alverson, USN (Ret.) entertained the gathering crowd.

J. Paul Trouche, president of the Palmetto Society, opened the ceremonies with a welcoming statement. Father James L. Parker, chaplain of the Maj. Gen. William Moultrie Chapter, gave the invocation. The Color Guard of the Washington Light Infantry presented the colors. The Charleston Community Band played *the Star Spangled Banner*, and those assembled sang along.

Gen. Rogers made opening remarks, including recognition of those instrumental in the successful completion of the project. Rogers and Vice Chairman Brailsford made special presentations to the Post and Courier Foundation, the Society of the Cincinnati, National Society of Colonial Wars and Charleston County Council.

Committee member and former South Carolina Gov. James Edwards formally presented the monument to Mayor Joseph P. Riley Jr. In his acceptance remarks, the Mayor spoke of the Battle of Sullivan's Island, the Declaration of Independence, and Moultrie's life before, during and after the American Revolution. In speaking of the bravery and dedication of our forefathers, Riley compared them to nine members of the Charleston Fire Department who had died in a blaze 10 days earlier.

The Right Rev. C. FitzSimons Allison, Bishop of South Carolina (Ret.), gave both the dedication and blessing. Trouche, Brailsford, Edwards and Riley tugged at four cords, releasing the blue drape covering the statue.

Five of the participating organizations — South Carolina Historical Society; Rebecca Motte Chapter, South Carolina Daughters of the American Revolution; Fort Sullivan Chapter, SCDAR; Sons of the American Revolution; and the Society of Cincinnati — one at a time laid wreaths at the monument's base. The laying of each wreath was punctuated by a cannon salute from the Waccamaw Light Infantry.

6. Defenders of Fort Sumter

The stalwart, classical figures immediately give notice that those being honored performed feats of near-mythic proportions.

The Details

The memorial is an allegorical depiction of the Confederate defense of Charleston during the War for Southern Independence. A young warrior clad in only a fig leaf and sandals holds a shield bearing the Seal of the State of South Carolina in his left hand and a short sword in his right. He represents the soldiers who manned Fort Sumter in defense of the city.

Charleston is personified not as a cowering Southern belle but as a defiant Amazon willing to share the pain and suffering of her young defender. There is a chain near her left foot, but she is unfettered. She holds laurel leaves, the warrior's reward. To continue the allegory: The seven steps leading from street level to the pedestal represent the states that formed the original Confederacy before the firing on

Fort Sumter drew Virginia, Arkansas, Tennessee and North Carolina into the Southern fold. The small, rough granite pieces around the pedestal are arranged in wave patterns. Further waves can be seen in the detail of the bronzes' base. However, it is here that the allegory ends. At the very bottom of the pedestal, a consistent pattern of alternating single and double stars can be seen, but symbolism is trumped by symmetry because the total equals 12, not the coveted 11 that could have represented all the states that eventually joined the Confederacy.

The 6-foot, 6-inch Bavarian granite pedestal is octagonal. The bronze figures stand 10-feet- 6-inches tall. The monument stands in the middle of a circular plaza with a 56½-foot diameter. Four concentric stone circles form a base for the pedestal and double as steps.

The sculptor, Hermon A. MacNeil (1866-1947) of Long Island, N.Y., (Inscription — H.A. MACNEIL — in the statue's base) was on hand for the 1932 dedication. Outside the art world, MacNeil was best known for designing the Standing Liberty quarter (1916-1930). But by 1932 his design had been superseded to commemorate the bicentennial of Washington's birth. The architect was Delano & Aldrich of New York. The Alexis Rudier Foundry of Paris (Inscription — Alexis RUDIER Fondeur PARIS — in the statue's base) cast the two bronze figures. The Dawson Engineering Company of Charleston performed the monument setting.

The monument is in the southeastern corner of the park, oriented toward the fort. The front of the pedestal bears the inscription.

TO THE
CONFEDERATE
DEFENDERS OF
CHARLESTON

_____

FORT SUMTER
1861—1865

Encircling the pedestal in bas-relief are heroic figures bearing sandbags to repair the fort's broken walls. Below is an encircling inscription: "Count them happy who for their faith and their courage endured a great fight."

On the inside of the low wall that partially surrounds the monument, there is a barely visible inscription:

THIS MONUMENT WAS ERECTED WITH FUNDS
BEQUEATHED BY ANDREW BUIST MURRAY IN
TRIBUTE TO THE CONFEDERATE DEFENDERS
OF FORT SUMTER.
MCMXXXII

Andrew Buist Murray (1844-1928), wealthy Charleston business-man and philanthropist, designated $100,000 in his will for "the erection of a suitable monument to the defenders of Fort Sumter." Murray Boulevard is named in his honor.

Use the smallest of the nearby live oaks as a landmark to find the inscription, which is on the interior portion of the wall nearest that tree.

Note the slots in the wall for drainage. They don't help much, and the plaza, like much of the Charleston peninsula, floods easily and frequently.

The total cost of the monument was between $80,000 to $90,000.

The History

At 4:30 a.m., April 12, 1861, a shell fired from James Island signaled the start of the Confederate attack on the Federal troops at Fort Sumter. Two days later the troops surrendered and left, and Confederate soldiers took possession of the fort. They occupied it until the Confederates evacuated Charleston on the night of February 17-18, 1865. During those roughly 46 months, Confederate soldiers tenaciously held the linchpin to Charleston's harbor.

On April 7, 1863, the U.S. Navy attacked the stronghold with a fleet of nine ironclads. All nine were heavily damaged and the *Keokuk* was lost. (See Dahlgren Gun — White Point Garden.)

During the summer of 1863, fierce fighting ensued on nearby Morris Island as the Union Army and Navy attempted to dislodge the Confederate defenders from strategic Battery Wagner. The Confederates finally abandoned their increasingly untenable position on September 7, 1863. Union guns were moved closer to Fort Sumter, by then a mere half mile away, and a fierce artillery barrage began.

On September 9, 1863, convinced that the prolonged bombardment had broken the Southerners' will to fight, the U.S. Navy

launched a landing force aboard small boats against Fort Sumter's shattered defenses. The alert garrison easily repelled the attackers, capturing more than a hundred prisoners.

Slowly but surely, Union artillery battered the fort into a pile of rubble, but during pauses in the shelling, men emerged from their hidey-holes and repaired as much damage as possible.

During the Union siege approximately 45,000 projectiles, weighing an estimated 3,500 tons, were fired into Sumter's fortifications. Despite the heavy bombardment, the casualties were astonishingly small — 52 killed and 267 wounded.

The Dedication

The Defenders of Fort Sumter monument was dedicated October 20, 1932. Mayor Burnet R. Maybank (1899-1954) closed all city offices to allow municipal employees the opportunity to attend the event.

Prior to the ceremonies, the Metz Band entertained the crowd of several thousand. David Huguenin, chairman of the Fort Sumter

Memorial Commission, was the master of ceremonies. The Right Rev. Albert S. Thomas, bishop of the Protestant Episcopal Church of South Carolina, gave the invocation.

The keynote speaker was Gerald White Johnson (1890-1980), author and editorial writer for the Baltimore Evening Sun. He lauded the gallant defense of the fort and urged those in attendance to adopt the same spirit in the fight against communism and fascism.

The Washington Light Infantry's Colonel W. Robert Greer, the only surviving Charlestonian from the Sumter garrison, paid tribute to the monument's benefactor Andrew Buist Murray. He also honored his fellow defenders, referring to Fort Sumter as "this great Gibraltar of Charleston."

Oliver J. Bond, vice chairman, introduced four young women — Emma Mayberry Walker, Lavinia Huguenin, Ann Stewart Barnwell and Camilla Floride Bissell — descendants of the stronghold's three commanders and engineer. As the band played the recessional, the young women unveiled the monument. At the same time, a Confederate flag was placed at the memorial's base. James R. Johnson of Charleston explained that it was the last to fly over Fort Sumter.

The band then struck up *Dixie*. Huguenin presented the monument to Mayor Maybank, who delivered an acceptance speech. The Most Rev. Emmet M. Walsh, bishop of the Roman Catholic Diocese of South Carolina, gave the benediction. As the ceremonies concluded, an honor guard, composed of men of Citadel Cadet Corps, the Washington Light Infantry and the Sumter Guards, escorted Greer and Stephen E. Welch, another Confederate veteran, from the site.

The Trivia

Fort Sumter was named for Revolutionary War hero General Thomas Sumter (1734-1832), nicknamed "The Gamecock," an allusion to his combative nature. After the Revolution he served in both the U.S. House and Senate. In an era not known for longevity, he died just months shy of his 98th birthday.

Fort Sumter was constructed on the "Middle Ground," a sandbar at the harbor's entrance. But before the fort could be built, an island had to be created to hold it. Initially, 10,000 tons of granite from the Penobscot River region of Maine were set in place, and an additional 60,000 tons of rock and stone were eventually laid atop that substructure until the site had an area of two-and-a-half acres.

7. Brooke Rifle

This double-banded 7-inch gun was the creation of John Mercer Brooke, one of those who armored the Union vessel *Merrimack,* thus creating the Confederate ironclad *Virginia.* On March 9, 1862, this ship famously clashed with the *Monitor,* a Union ironclad, off Hampton Roads, Va. The gun was manufactured at the Confederate Naval Ordnance Works at Selma, Ala. Catesby ap Roger Jones — "ap" is a Welsh patronymic, meaning "son of" — operated the foundry. Jones' initials — C ap R — can be seen on one trunnion and the marking VII in can be seen in two locations.

Recovered from Fort Johnson on James Island in 1900, the gun was subsequently mounted in the park.

8. Defenders of Fort Moultrie

Despite the many plaques and inscriptions, the onlooker's focus is quickly drawn upward to the young Revolutionary War soldier.

The Details

The monument is popularly referred to as the Jasper Monument, but its official name is The Defenders of Fort Moultrie. The name is anachronistic. At the time of the battle, the incomplete fort was either unnamed or called Fort Sullivan. Only after the victory was it quickly renamed in honor of Colonel William Moultrie, the commanding officer. Although the monument is dedicated to all the South Carolina militiamen involved in the battle, the statue clearly depicts Sergeant William Jasper in heroic pose and clad in his regimental uniform, his right hand pointing across the harbor to the battle site, his left holding his regimental flag.

The statue and pedestal stand on a knoll, which is edged in concrete, with brick walkways on the east and west opening on a 16-foot, 4-inch square brick plaza. The area not covered with brick is planted in Asiatic jasmine. The granite base is 15 feet high; the statue itself is described as 6 feet, 6 inches ("The Battery — Charleston, South Carolina"). A cannonball is at each of the extremities of the brick plaza as you approach from the east.

Each of the monument's faces has bronze plaques and/or inscriptions:

SOUTH — The highest bronze plaque lists the officers and artillerists of the 2nd South Carolina Regiment.

The lower plate is a bas-relief of the Seal of the State of South Carolina. The male and female figures and the angel are a framework for, but not part of, the seal. The actual seal is made up of two side-by-side ellipses. They touch in the middle, and are linked at the top and bottom by palmetto fronds. The left half of the seal shows a palmetto growing from a fallen oak, representing the South Carolina victory over the British fleet. Lying against the palmetto's trunk, in the shape of an "X", are two banded bundles of six spears each, representing the first 12 states to form the United States.*

Not shown in the bas-relief is the motto: QUIS SEPARABIT?, meaning "Who will separate?" Hanging on the palmetto are what appear to be two pineapples. Even accounting for artistic license and calling them coconuts would still be inaccurate because palmettos yield large clusters of berries. In fact, being represented are two shields, except some details are missing, two dates — March 26 and July 4. Both commemorate significant events in 1776.

The first is the date of South Carolina's first independent constitution. The second is the date that the Second Continental Congress approved the text of the Declaration of Independence. ANIMIS OPIBUSQUE PARAT translates to "Prepared in mind and resources."

The right half of the seal features a woman walking along a beach strewn with weapons. She represents hope, and the laurel in her hand

and the rising sun behind her symbolize the victory at the Battle of Sullivan's Island. DUM SPIRO SPERO translates to "While I breathe, I hope." SPES is the noun form of "Hope."

EAST — The highest bronze plate gives the date the 2nd South Carolina Regiment of Foot was organized: June 17, 1775.

The lower bronze plate is the dedication: "TO THE DEFENDERS OF FORT MOULTRIE JUNE THE 28TH, 1776". The dedication is enclosed by a wreath composed of oak (left) and laurel (right), signifying strength and glory, respectively.

Below the bronze there is an inscription of a laudatory statement by General Charles Lee, overall commander of the American forces in Charlestown at the time of the battle.

And below that another inscription: ERECTED UNDER THE AUSPICES OF THE PALMETTO GUARD JUNE 28, 1876. (Actually a year later, as you'll soon see.)

WEST — The top bronze lists those killed in the battle.

Below that a bronze bas-relief depicts Jasper's heroism. Just below the bas-relief, inscribed in the granite, is a quote attributed to Jasper: "DON'T LET US FIGHT WITHOUT A FLAG."

NORTH — The upper plate lists the names of the wounded, including Sergeant Young — John Young!

The lower bronze bas-relief features the Seal of the City of Charleston, or rather the seal as it appeared in 1877. In the foreground, there is a seated female figure, her right arm raised and pointing. Her left arm is lowered and her left hand should be holding a staff. Look carefully and you can see a pin where the staff was once attached. A liberty cap should be hanging on the staff.

Above the woman is the city's motto: AEDES MORES JURAQUE CURAT. The Latin phrase translates to: "She cares for her temples, customs and rights." On the left, a ship is under full sail. In the background is a water view of the city, although the number of Byzantine domes on the skyline has been slightly exaggerated. At the very bottom, there is another Latin phrase: CORPUS POLITICUM, meaning "body politic."

Viett Marble Works completed the stonework. "E.T. Viett" (Emile T. Viett) appears in the lower right hand corner of the Jasper quote, and "E.T. Viett 1876" can be seen in the short base just below the statue. The George Fisher & Co. of New York completed the bronze castings. The estimated cost of all the work was $10,000.

* On July 2, 1776, when the delegates at the Second Continental Congress voted on the issue of independence, the vote was 12-0-1 with 12 states in favor, none in opposition, and New York abstaining. Hence, 12 spears! New York's legislature had not granted its delegation the mandate to take that final step. On July 19, 1776, Congress received notification that New York's legislature had voted in support of independence, making the matter unanimous.

The Biographical Sketch

William Jasper (ca.1750-1779) enlisted in the 2nd South Carolina Regiment of Foot as a private in Halifax District, Ga., on July 7, 1775, rapidly rising to the rank of sergeant. The actions that propelled him into the history books, according to his commander Colonel William Moultrie, were: "Sergeant Jasper perceiving that the flag (regimental) was shot away, and had fallen without the fort, jumped from one of the embrasures and brought it up through a heavy fire, fixed it upon a spunge-staff,* and planted it upon the ramparts again."

The next day, in acknowledgement of his bravery, President (Governor) John Rutledge offered Jasper his personal sword and a commission. Jasper accepted the sword but declined the commission, feeling his lack of education would prove an embarrassment to his men. Soon afterward he became a backwoods scout, a service for which he was well suited, according to another commander, General Benjamin Lincoln. On October 9, 1779, during the Siege of Savannah, in a scene oddly reminiscent of his moment of glory, Jasper attempted to rescue the regimental colors on the Spring Hill redoubt, but was hit in the chest by musket fire and killed.

* Sponge staff — A long pole with a wool-covered "sponge" head, used for cleaning and extinguishing sparks in the cannon's bore between shots.

The History

At 10 a.m., June 28, 1776, the British Army and Navy attacked the American forces, mostly South Carolina militiamen, on Sullivan's Island. The army was thwarted in its attempts to attack the northern end of the island from its positions on Long Island (Isle of Palms). The navy fared little better in its efforts to reduce the partially completed palmetto-log-and-sand fort on the southern end. When the fighting ended 10 hours later, the British Navy had suffered more than 200 casualties, heavy damage to a number of ships and the loss of the

28-gun vessel *Actaeon*. The South Carolina militiamen suffered only 37 casualties. With the British withdrawal, the Battle of Sullivan's Island marked an early American victory in the Revolutionary War.

The Dedication

The Palmetto Guard dedicated the memorial June 28, 1877, not June 28, 1876, as the monument's plaque indicates. The June 28, 1876, edition of the News and Courier featured a conjectural drawing of the monument, but in fact, the South Carolina granite base was the only structure on site in time for the centennial.

Leading up to the 1877 dedication ceremonies, the Palmetto Guard and honored guests made an excursion to Middleton Place. Returning to the city, a parade was organized. The Palmetto Guard and 11 other state and local military organizations wended their way to White Point. The Rev. W.H. Campbell, rector of St. Luke's, opened the ceremonies with a prayer. General B.H. Rutledge gave the oration. In the absence of Governor Wade Hampton, Captain C.R. Holmes, monument committee chairman, unveiled the memorial.

It somehow seems appropriate that the monument wasn't completed in time for the centennial because, after all, neither was the fort at the time of the battle.

9. Fake Four-Pounder

Unlike the other guns in the park, this cannon was never part of a military battle but rather a political one.

In 1933 this cannon was created after a contentious fight between city officials and the residents of Longitude Lane concerning the ownership of a British four-pounder buried there. After the city took possession of the gun and mounted it at White Point, a practical joker built the replica and dropped it off at Longitude Lane. The neighborhood was not amused and it also ended up in the park.

Although it looks real, the "cannon" is cast around a pipe to avoid the difficulty of drilling out the center. Note the "HF" inscription, a feeble attempt to connect the gun with the Revolutionary era Hill Foundry in York, S.C.

In 1993 the authentic British four-pounder, one near the park's pathway across from Church Street, was vandalized, then removed for repairs. Subsequently, it disappeared in a still unsolved case. A plaque marks its former location.

Speaking of things missing, at the corner of South Battery and King streets, there is an empty pedestal. An American-made 1851 bronze howitzer* once stood there, but unlike the four-pounder, it has not mysteriously disappeared but rather is safely among the collections of the Charleston Museum at 360 Meeting Street.

* Both howitzers and mortars are short cannon with a low muzzle velocity used in firing shells in a relatively high trajectory.

10. Thirteen-Inch Mortars

There are four of these guns in the park. They are 13-inch Sea-coast Mortars, Model 1861, manufactured by the Fort Pitt Foundry, Pittsburgh, Pa. Note inscriptions or partial inscriptions — Fort Pitt PA 1861 17100 lbs D.W.F. No 30. Each weighs approximately 17,100 pounds. The guns had a range of nearly three miles and fired a 218-pound spherical shell. Ten-inch cannonballs are stacked in pyramids near the mortars.

11. Simms Memorial

The bust's stern gaze is softened by its tousled hair, giving insight into the multi-faceted nature of William Gilmore Simms.

The Details

The bronze bust of Simms, noted Charleston writer, was the work of J.Q.A. (John Quincy Adams) Ward (1830-1910) of New York. Note his name and "sculptor" on the left shoulder of the bust. On the right shoulder, note "Geo. Fischer & Bro. Bronze Foundry N.Y." — the same company that completed the bronze elements on the Defenders of Fort Moultrie monument.

Edward Brickell White, antebellum Charleston architect who relocated to New York after the Late Unpleasantness, designed the Winnsboro granite pedestal. T.W. Woodward, J.H. Rion and J.B. McCants of Winnsboro, S.C., contributed the stone. Viett Marble Works of Charleston completed the stonework. Inscribed low on the pedestal is the dedication date — June 11, 1879.

The monument stands on an octagonal brick plaza. The 10-foot pedestal is mostly Winnsboro granite but the lowest portion is brick. The bust is 3 feet, 6 inches tall.

During his heyday, Simms was considered the antebellum South's leading man of letters. The pedestal originally bore only his surname SIMMS in Roman block letters with polished surfaces. As his fame faded in the 20th century, however, an inscription was added: William Gilmore Simms, 1806-1870, Author, Journalist, Historian.

The Biography

William Gilmore Simms (1806-1870) was born in Charleston, the son of William and Harriet Ann Singleton Simms. His mother died when he was an infant and his maternal grandmother primarily raised him. Although he always claimed his education was deficient, he did attend the city schools for four years and the College of Charleston an additional two. Regardless, most of his education was acquired through his insatiable reading and keen observation. In 1825 he began to study law, and by the following year was admitted to the bar. At the same time he began to pursue his writing. He founded and edited the Album, a weekly literary journal, often filling it with his own prolific output. On October 19, 1826, he married Anna Malcolm Giles. In 1829 he became editor of the City Gazette.

In the early 1830s Simms experienced a series of personal losses. His wife died, leaving him with a 4-year-old daughter; both his father and grandmother died; and his Summerville home burned.

Soon afterward, Simms resigned his editorship and went to New York to further his literary career. His time was well spent meeting fellow writers, editors and publishers. Upon his return to Charleston, he was determined to make his living as a professional writer. In three years time, Harper and Brothers of New York published "Martin Faber" (1833), "Guy Rivers" (1834), "the Yemassee" (1835) and "the Partisan" (1835). These works were widely read and well reviewed, establishing Simms' literary reputation.

Simms soon became the city's best-known author, publishing a seemingly endless string of essays, reviews, poems, histories and novels. During this period, his novels were considered the equal of those by Sir Walter Scott and James Fenimore Cooper. The books were historical fiction, termed "romances" at the time. His actual historical work included a state history (a revised version of which was used by South Carolina schoolchildren well into the late 1950s) and biographies of Captain John Smith, General Nathanael Greene and General Francis Marion.

Simms' personal life brightened with his marriage to Chevilette Roach, daughter of a wealthy planter. The couple had 14 children, only five surviving to adulthood. He and his new wife took up residence at Woodlands, one of the Roach family plantations near Orangeburg. However, poor financial management by his father-in-law required Simms to write almost constantly to make ends meet. Despite his love of rural life, he frequently resided at his townhouse in Charleston, where he presided over the city's literary circle.

Simms had a political career as well, first holding the office of magistrate, later serving in the South Carolina General Assembly, and in 1846, narrowly losing a race for lieutenant governor. He was a Unionist during the Nullification Crisis but gradually became a Secessionist. Once converted, his writings marked him as a major and outspoken advocate for and defender of the Southern cause. Some view his novel "Woodcraft" as a rebuttal of "Uncle Tom's Cabin." In 1856, during a Northern lecture tour, his strong attacks on the anti-slavery movement led to harsh criticism of his own politics and an abrupt severance of many of his Yankee ties.

Simms' personal losses were devastating during the Lost Cause. His townhouse in Charleston was destroyed, Woodlands burned in an accidental fire and Sherman's forces destroyed what had been rebuilt. His second wife and several of his children died, and he was in Columbia when the capital burned.

After the war, despite an impressive volume of writing, Simms was never able to revive his literary career.

The History and Dedication

In 1872 the effort to honor Simms began with the organization of the Simms Memorial Association and the election of W.D. Porter as chairman. Later, William Cullen Bryant, 19th century poet and journalist and an old friend of Simms, recommended sculptor J.Q.A. Ward to the association. Ward reduced his customary commission from $2,000 to $1,700. The Carolina Art Association joined forces with the Simms Memorial Association to further the cause.

The memorial was dedicated June 11, 1879, the ninth anniversary of the writer's death. A large assemblage gathered in White Point Garden, including the Board of Control of the Confederate Home and the officers and members of the Simms Memorial Association and the Carolina Art Association. Among the distinguished guests were Mayor W.W. Sale, the Board of Aldermen, Judge T.B. Fraser, the Rev. Edward R. Miles, the Rev. C.C. Pinckney and Mrs. Edward Roach, Simms' daughter.

At 5 p.m., Professor N.R. Middleton, president of the Carolina Art Association, announced the opening of the ceremonies. The Rev. Mr. Miles gave an opening prayer. Middleton acknowledged the many letters of congratulations received. J.P.K. Bryan, secretary of the Carolina Art Association, read several of them. Middleton spoke of the concerted efforts required to achieve the goal of honoring Simms.

At the conclusion of Middleton's remarks, Chevilette and Annie Teft Roach, Simms' granddaughters, and two young ladies from the Confederate Home, all dressed in "spotless" white outfits, drew on four cords, allowing the state flag that served as a drape to be gracefully hoisted to the top of a temporary flagpole and unveiled the bust.

Colonel James Armstrong then read a letter from the students at the Confederate Home. They contributed a laurel wreath for the ceremony. Armstrong placed the wreath upon the bust's brow.

Professor Middleton then introduced W.D. Porter, chairman of the Simms Memorial Association and principal speaker. In his oration Porter praised the writer's work: "The prose style of Simms is manly, nervous, flexible and dramatic. He has a complete mastery of the resources of the English language. There is a vein of poetry in his prose style, which, without inflating or exaggerating it, makes it buoyant and charming."

Middleton then presented the memorial to the City of Charleston. Accepting, Mayor Sale said, "It now, sir, remains for me to assure you that we will guard this precious gift with sacred vigilance, valuing it as our choicest treasure."

12. Williams Music Pavilion

The bandstand evokes an earlier, simpler time when crowds gathered for a Sunday concert in the park.

The Details

Note the inscription in the pavilion's rafters: IN MEMORIAM—M.F.W.—APRIL 1905. The initials are those of Martha Fort Porter Williams (1831-1905). Also shown are the month and year of her death. She was the wife of wealthy banker and merchant George W. Williams. In her own right, she was known for her relief and charitable work and her horticultural talents. The bandstand is a rarity in the major downtown parks, one of only three memorials dedicated to women.

Following Mrs. Williams' death, her daughter Martha "Mattie" Wade Williams Carrington (1867-1930) contracted for the pavilion's construction. It was placed at the intersection of two of the park's walkways. The octagonal structure's architect was William Martin Aiken (1855-1908), a Charleston native, living in New York at the time.

Charleston contractor Robert McArtney began work in the fall of 1906 and despite some delays in obtaining the proper building materials, completed the structure the following year at a cost of $5,000.

In 1934 the floor was raised three feet to accommodate restrooms, which are long gone now. The Hardman Development Co. completed a major restoration of the pavilion during 1984-85. Additional work, including painting, was completed in 2006.

In 2009, as part of White Point Garden's overall rehabilitation, the city awarded a $273,500 contract to Charles Blanchard Construction Corporation of North Charleston. During 2009 and into early 2010, another major restoration was undertaken. The old floor and foundation were demolished to return the structure to its original height — three feet above grade. Four steps, with handrails, lead to the new 25-foot-by-25-foot cement floor on two sides. The floor peaks in the middle to promote drainage. An iron railing encloses the floor.

Eight 12-foot fluted cast-iron columns topped with Corinthian capitals support an iron arcade. Near the base of each column, the name "J.F. Riley Ironworks" (a Charleston foundry) can be seen. Atop the iron truss work rests a wooden framework, which supports a green tiled roof capped with a terra cotta pineapple finial.

Biographical Sketches

Martha Fort Porter married George Walton Williams (1820-1903) on November 4, 1856, in Madison, Ga. It was a double wedding; her sister Sally married Azariah Graves in the same ceremony.

This was Williams' second marriage. His phenomenal success in business was counterbalanced by his tragic personal life. In 1854 he, his first wife Louisa and their children moved from Augusta, Ga., to Charleston to expand his business enterprises. Over the next three years, Louisa and all five children (ranging in age from two weeks to nine years) died from a variety of causes.

Once remarried, George had six children with Martha, four of whom lived to adulthood. By 1876 the family was living at 16 Meeting Street (now called the Calhoun Mansion), a grand Victorian structure reputed to have cost $200,000 to construct. Mattie was the Williamses' youngest daughter. On June 11, 1890, she married

Charleston jeweler Waring Parker Carrington (1849-1937). It was the social event of the season; 2,500 wedding invitations were sent out. The ceremonies were held at the Trinity Methodist Church. The bridal party consisted of 13 couples, and guests attended from across the country. By 1892 Mattie and Waring had completed construction of their Queen Anne style home at 2 Meeting Street, overlooking White Point Garden.

Dedication

Despite intermittent rain, the Williams Music Pavilion was dedicated June 28, 1907— Carolina Day. The Metz Military Band performed the inaugural concert on the bandstand.

Today, wedding ceremonies are far more common than band performances. A city permit to use the facility typically costs $95 to $200, but the maximum allowable size of a wedding party is only 25. Certainly, then, no weddings on the site are ever going to eclipse that of the Carringtons.

13. The Little Dancer

An elfin girl in a frolicsome mood kicks at a stream of water bubbling up from the basin below.

A Brief History and Details

On April 25, 1962, Mayor J. Palmer Gaillard (1920-2006) presented a model of "the Little Dancer," a work of Charleston sculptor Willard Hirsch, to the Board of Parks. The bronze sculpture and drinking fountain were a gift to Charleston if the city would pay for the installation of water pipes and drainage. After some discussion, the board approved acceptance of the gift and authorized Gaillard to express thanks to the donor, Sarah "Sallie" Carrington Chaney, daughter of Mattie and Waring Carrington. (See White Point Garden—Williams Music Pavilion.) Chaney also contributed money for the descriptive plaques and brick aprons for the park's cannon. In 1962 the bronze was cast in New York and erected in the park. Hirsch had created the Little Dancer in the late 1940s, and the original served as the model for some 20 bronze castings scattered about the country. The cost of the fountain was approximately $850.

Hirsch inscribed the bottom edge of the back of the little girl's skirt with his signature, the date "1962" and the words, "Given to

the children of Charleston by a friend."

The work is situated on a 7-foot square brick plaza. The 20-inch bronze stands atop a 20-inch stone pedestal that contains the octagonal drinking fountain. Both stand on a 3-foot-by-3-foot granite base standing 6 inches high.

The Sculptor

Willard Newman Hirsch (1905-1982) was descended from a Jewish family that settled in the Charleston area in 1798. He studied at the College of Charleston for one year (1923), but when his father died, he quit to help support his family.

During the Depression, he was unable to find work in Charleston. So at the age of 28, with the encouragement of relatives in New York City, he moved there. Still unable to secure steady employment, he decided to pursue his love of art, winning a scholarship to the National Academy of Design.

Sculpture became his passion. He continued his studies at the Beaux Arts Institute. He maintained a studio in New York City for 10 years. In 1945 after completing two years service in the Army, he returned to the city of his birth. Over the years, he taught at the College of Charleston, Gibbes Museum of Art and the extension campuses of both Furman University and the University of South Carolina.

Hirsch exhibited extensively during his career, including the Pennsylvania Academy of Fine Arts, Whitney Museum of American Art, National Sculpture Gallery, Metropolitan Museum of Art, the New York World's Fair, Brooks Memorial Gallery and Corcoran Gallery of Art.

Much of Hirsch's work is on permanent public display in Charleston. One of his bronze sculptures, "Dancing Children," is in Washington Square. "The Cassique of Kiawah" is on the grounds of Charles Towne Landing State Park, west of the Ashley River. A bronze bust of Mayor J. Palmer Gaillard is on display, appropriately enough, in the lobby of the Gaillard Auditorium at 77 Calhoun Street. Hirsch also completed the bust of Congressman L. Mendel Rivers at the entrance of the O.T. Wallace County Office Building at 101 Meeting Street.

Three pieces of Hirsch's art are on the second floor of Charleston's Main Library at 68 Calhoun Street: "Readers" in the lobby; "Lamp of Learning" near the entrance of the Gallery; and "Alice in Wonderland" at the entrance of the Children's Library. In 1961 the pieces were donated by the Home Federal Savings and Loan Association and served as exterior features of the Old Library at 404 King Street. Before the new library opened, Anita and Jerry Zucker provided funds for refurbishment and installation.

Kahal Kadosh Beth Elohim, the nation's first Reform Jewish Congregation, at 90 Hasell Street, has two of Hirsch's works on display: "the Prophet of Hope" and "Consolation and the Prophet of Admonition."

14. Amberjack Memorial

A simple monument honors the ultimate sacrifice of World War II submariners.

The Details

The memorial holds two bronze plaques. The higher of the two has a bas-relief of a submarine. It recognizes the 52 American submarines and their 3,505 crew members lost during World War II. There are quotes by Fleet Admiral Chester Nimitz and Commander Submarine Force Vice Admiral C.A. Lockwood Jr. The second plaque lists the 72 crewmembers of the *Amberjack* and their ranks (officers) or rates and ratings (enlisted personnel). A square brick pad holds a 9-inch base and a 7-foot-tall granite memorial. E.J. McCarthy & Sons Monument Co. created and erected it. The memorial cost $1,400 to construct.

The History

The submarine *Amberjack (SS-219)* was launched March 6, 1942, in Groton, Conn. (Amberjack is the name of three species of Atlantic fish of the Carangidae family.) She was commissioned June 19 and left for the Pacific in August.

On her first patrol in September/October 1942, she sank two Japanese merchant ships. During the invasion of Guadalcanal, she became the only U.S. submarine to be used as a cargo ship, transporting 9,000 gallons of aviation fuel, two hundred 100-pound bombs and 17 American flyers.

On her second patrol, she was depth-charged by a Japanese surface ship, but later inflicted undetermined damage on another enemy vessel.

During her last patrol, she made contact with an enemy submarine and sank a twin-masted schooner by gunfire. On February 4, 1943, she attacked a heavily armed munitions ship on the surface, sustaining casualties. After submerging, she retaliated with a salvo of five torpedoes, reportedly sinking the vessel.

The *Amberjack's* last radio communication occurred February 14, when she reported evading two Japanese destroyers and later picking up a downed enemy pilot. She may have been lost February 16, when Japanese war records indicate that their aircraft bombed an unidentified American submarine in the area of last contact.

Subsequently, Japanese vessels reported observing large amounts of oil and parts of a submarine hull. Despite the uncertainty of her fate, *Amberjack* became one of 52 American submarines lost during the war, or using Navy terminology, "still on patrol."

Although the submarine had no connections to Charleston when the Swamp Fox Chapter, Submarine Veterans of World War II was organized in 1968, the *Amberjack* was designated as the Charleston chapter's "state ship." Confusion arose when a second *Amberjack (SS-522)* made Charleston her home port.

The Dedication

On May 23, 1970, the Swamp Fox Chapter unveiled the Amberjack Memorial. Lieutenant Commander P.V. Hansen recounted the history of the submarine. Rear Admiral James B. Osborne was the main speaker. Mayor J. Palmer Gaillard accepted the memorial on behalf of the city. The crew of the second *Amberjack (SS-522)* also participated in the ceremonies.

15. Hobson Monument

From a distance, the monument is reminiscent of a ship's prow or a massive gravestone. Up close, one quickly realizes that it is both.

The Details

The American Institute for Commemorative Art of New York designed the monument for the USS Hobson Memorial Society. The main monolith, the curbing and the nearby benches are all composed of pink granite from quarries near Salisbury, N.C. Claude

W. Brown Memorials of Florence, S.C., erected the monument. The City of Charleston funded and constructed the substantial foundation. The shaft's height is 20 feet (April 2, 1954 — The Charleston Evening Post).

The monument's circular raised plaza, edged with curved cuts of stone, is 23 feet in diameter. It's a mosaic of different types of stone in various shapes. Some of the stones are inscribed with state names or abbreviations. Some are not. In two instances, the inscriptions read, "Charleston, S.C." A metal arrow appears to pierce the base of the monument, bearing the site of the peacetime accident that sank the ship — Latitude 42 degrees, 21 minutes North, Longitude 44 degrees, 15 minutes West.

The side facing Murray Boulevard bears a sundial with a bronze gnomon, which is a blade-like structure that casts a shadow. The sundial is inscribed with the date and time of the sinking. Below are the sailors' names in alphabetical order along with their ranks or rates and ratings. Ages and places of residence are also included. Twelve South Carolinians died in the tragedy, five of them Charlestonians.

The side facing South Battery Street features an inscribed portrait of the destroyer-minesweeper *Hobson (DMS-26)* sinking. Below the portrait are inscriptions of both accident and dedication details. The inscription indicates that the plaza stones came from each of the 38 home states of those lost. In fact, though, the sailors came from 36 different states, the District of Columbia and the Province of Ontario. There are more than 176 stones but some have obviously been inserted to fill gaps. The monument's cost was $17,000.

The History

The *Hobson's* keel was laid in November 1940 at the Charleston Naval Shipyard and she was stationed in Charleston at the time of her sinking.

She was named for Rear Admiral Richard Pearson Hobson (1870-1937), hero of the Spanish-American War, Medal of Honor winner and Congressman.

During World War II, the *Hobson (DD-464)*, a Gleaves-class destroyer, was involved in the invasions of North Africa, Sicily, Normandy and southern France. She also escorted convoys across the Atlantic, and on March 13, 1944, helped sink a German submarine.

In November 1944, once again in the Charleston Naval Shipyard, she was converted to a destroyer-minesweeper and reclassified (DMS-26). Sent to the Pacific Theater, she participated in the American invasion of Okinawa. During kamikaze attacks, a bomb damaged her and four crew members died. Nonetheless, her crew brought down several enemy planes. That was the ship's last action. She was sent to the Norfolk Naval Shipyard for repairs. On November 21, 1948, she was assigned to Charleston.

On April 26, 1952, at 10:26 p.m., while on maneuvers 700 miles west of the Azores, the American aircraft carrier *Wasp* struck the *Hobson* amidships, shearing her in half. The *Hobson* went down in less than four minutes, taking eight officers and 168 enlisted men with her. It was one of the Navy's worst peacetime disasters.

The Dedication

The USS Hobson Memorial Society, composed of shipmates, relatives and friends, dedicated the monument on Sunday, April 25, 1954, a day before the second anniversary of the disaster. A crowd estimated at 2,500, including military personnel, attended.

The ceremonies began with the arrival of the Sixth Naval District Band and the Palmetto Post 112, American Legion Drum and Bugle Corps. Next, 600 officers and men of the Atlantic Fleet Mine Force formed ranks on Murray Boulevard, creating a sea of white. Two young children who lost their fathers in the accident — Audrea Milton, daughter of Chief Quartermaster Carl C. Milton, and James R. Moss III, son of storekeeper James R. Moss Jr. — tugged at the lines that released the canvas cover.

Lieutenant Commander F.A. Adams, a Navy chaplain, gave the invocation. Commander (Ret.) Edward P. Brennan, president of the Hobson Society and father of Radioman John J. Brennan, introduced the distinguished guests.

Mayor William McG. Morrison, delivering the welcoming address, declared, "This is perhaps the most serious moment I shall witness in my tenure of office. It particularly saddens the hearts of Charleston folk."

Commander Brennan outlined the reasons for the society's formation. Rear Admiral Harry Sanders, commander of Atlantic Mine Fleet, spoke of the heroism on that fateful night. Navy Captain J. Lloyd Dreith, acting chief of chaplains, delivered the memorial address.

Following the address, Commander J.H. Floyd, former *Hobson* commander, and Mrs. Edward J. O'Neill, mother of Seaman Apprentice Edward J. O'Neill Jr., placed a gold star-shaped wreath at the monument's base. As the wreath was placed, Lieutenant R.B. Conneau sang the *Navy Hymn*.

A few minutes later, as a bugler sounded Taps, the Navy vessel *Tumult*, anchored just off the Battery, fired a three-gun salute. The ceremonies ended with a benediction by Rabbi Louis A. Weintraub, auxiliary Jewish chaplain. Relatives and friends were transported in small boats to the Navy vessel *Jeffers* for a wreath-laying at sea. While these ceremonies were taking place, twelve Navy Cougar jets, stationed in Jacksonville, Fla., flew overhead in an "H" formation.

Following the ceremonies at sea, the second annual meeting of the USS Hobson Memorial Society was held at the hall of the Palmetto American Legion, Post 112.

Memorial services are still held annually on the Sunday nearest the anniversary of the disaster.

16. World War I Howitzer

This is the most modern gun in the park. Markings identify it as a 9.2-inch Howitzer, Model 1917, M-1, manufactured by the Bethlehem Steel Company in 1918.

17. French Cannon

This Revolutionary-era four-pounder (cannonball size) was placed in the park in the early 1900s. The *fleur-de-lis* clearly identifies it as a French gun. A gift from the Andrew Simonds family, it was recovered from the Camden, S.C., battlefield, site of British General Lord Cornwallis' August 16, 1780, victory over American forces led by General Horatio Gates.

18. USS Maine Capstan

In early 2007 the battleship *Maine's* capstan was removed from its site in White Point to make way for the William Moultrie statue. A capstan is an upright, spool-shaped cylinder that is turned on an inner shaft by machinery or hand, and around which cables or hawsers are wound to raise or lower anchors.

After some conservation work, the current plan calls for the capstan's return and placement on the site of the vacated base at the corner of King and South Battery streets.

The Details

The capstan's base in White Point was deemed to have no major historic significance, so it was not conserved. A new base has not yet been designed. Three brass tablets, cast by J.F. Riley Ironworks of Charleston, were affixed to the original base. One plate described the *Maine's* sinking and the resulting 266 deaths. The second described the donation of the capstan to the city. The third delineated the removal from Hampton Park and relocation to White Point. The July

16, 1927, edition of the News and Courier reported: "The tablet for the west side will be placed later." Although there was a fourth set of bolts, there apparently never was a fourth plate. That might change with the latest string of events.

The History

On the night of February 15, 1898, an explosion ripped open the *Maine,* and the American battleship slowly settled to the bottom of Cuba's Havana harbor. Two officers and 258 men were killed outright. Although responsibility was never pinpointed, this incident ignited the Spanish-American War, or as the Spanish term it: *el Desastre del 98.* It also gave American forces the rallying cry: "Remember the *Maine!*"

In 1910 Congress, responding to growing public pressure, authorized the financing of a project to raise the ship. A cofferdam — a watertight chamber attached to the side of a ship to facilitate repairs below the water line — was submerged around the vessel and by November 2, 1911, the hull was exposed. The stern, the only part not completely shattered by the blast, was made watertight and on February 13, 1912, two days short of the 14th anniversary of the sinking, this section was refloated. On March 16, 1912, the remains of the battleship were towed out to sea and, after appropriate ceremonies, sunk in 600 fathoms of water.

Various recovered relics were distributed to states, municipalities and military organizations throughout the nation. In May 1913 U.S. Senator Benjamin R. Tillman of South Carolina obtained a cannon — still mounted on the State House grounds in Columbia — and the capstan.

Originally mounted in Hampton Park, the capstan gradually deteriorated. In 1927 the Victor Blue Camp, No. 6, United Spanish War Veterans had it reconditioned at the Naval Shipyard in North Charleston.

The Dedication

On July 15, 1927 Mayor Thomas P. Stoney and City Council were among the approximately 500 people who witnessed the unveiling of the refurbished capstan and the presentation of three new plaques to the city.

The United States Navy Yard Band opened the ceremonies with the playing of *America*. The Rev. Harold Thomas, rector of St. Luke's Episcopal Church, made the invocation. John C. Catherwood, commander of the Victor Blue Camp, presented the tablets to Mayor Stoney. In his remarks, Catherwood said, "One of the fundamental purposes of the United Spanish War Veterans is to perpetuate the deeds and memories of the comrades of the war with Spain. A second purpose is to instill into the minds of Americans a strong sense of patriotism."

In his acceptance speech, Mayor Stoney recounted the events that brought the capstan to Charleston. The other principal speakers were Charles S. Glover, commander, Charleston Post No. 11, American Legion; and G.L. Buist Rivers, representing the Chamber of Commerce. Glover observed, "The Spanish American War marked the birth of national consciousness. It obliterated sectionalism and brought men closer together." Mercedes Catherwood performed the unveiling. The Rev. James J. May, rector of St. John the Baptist Roman Catholic Cathedral, gave the benediction. The Navy Yard Band ended the occasion with *the Star Spangled Banner.*

The Trivia

The United States declared war on Spain April 25, 1898. On December 10, 1898, the Treaty of Paris ended the Spanish-American War. Spain ceded Puerto Rico, the Philippines and Guam to the

United States. The United States also took temporary control of Cuba, transitioning the country to independence in 1902.

19. Rapid-Fire Gun

Possibly a trophy of the Spanish-American War, this weapon features five barrels and may have been mounted on a ship. The markings, not presently visible, are Spanish and indicate it was manufactured in 1886. However, the gun's mount is American-made. It seems highly unlikely that these two elements were ever actually joined to create a functional weapon. Palmetto Post 112, American Legion presented it to the city in 1937.

Marion Square

Unlike most parks, Marion Square is not quiet and sedate, particularly during the school year when its proximity to the College of Charleston makes it a major gathering place for students.

Marion Square

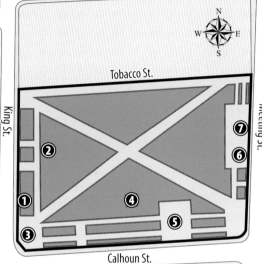

Hutson St.

Tobacco St.

King St.

Meeting St.

Calhoun St.

Key for map and descriptions that follow

1. Marion Square Plaque
2. Hornwork Section
3. Charleston Rotary Fountain
4. Calhoun Monument
5. Charleston Holocaust Memorial
6. Cast Iron Fountain
7. Hampton Obelisk

Photo at left shows the Hornwork, a remnant of a wall erected to protect the city during the American Revolution, in the background is the statue honoring John C. Calhoun.

The Location

Marion Square is a 6.85-acre park, bound by Tobacco, Meeting, Calhoun and King streets.

The History

The park is named for Revolutionary War hero General Francis Marion (1732-1795), nicknamed the "Swamp Fox." Although he was an officer in the Continental Army, he was one of the South Carolina militia leaders who tormented the British and Loyalist forces through a combination of mobility and surprise. Referred to as partisan fighting during the Revolution, they are strategies of modern guerrilla warfare.

During the Revolution, "The Lines," the city's northern defenses, and the "Hornwork," the fortifications that protected the city gates on King Street, stood on the site of this park.

When the city was incorporated in 1783, the state passed title of the property to the municipal government. A tobacco market developed just beyond the property's northern boundary between Hutson and Tobacco streets, which is no longer a thoroughfare today.

After a slave uprising conspiracy (Denmark Vesey plot) was uncovered in 1822, the city built an arsenal just north of the present site of Tobacco Street.

In 1833 the city conveyed the property to the Field Officers of the Fourth Brigade, provided that the land was kept open as "a public mall and parade ground for the use of the militia of the Charleston regiments and citizens forever."

By 1842 the arsenal, commonly called the "citadel," became the first home of the Military College of South Carolina — the Citadel.

By 1856 the square was in deplorable condition. The city and field officers sought to improve the grounds and purchase some remaining building lots. However, the Brothers' War put most of those plans on hold.

In 1876 the city conveyed additional property to the field officers. In 1882 City Council named the park Marion Square and set up a seven-member commission to oversee the administration and improvements. Today the Washington Light Infantry and the Sumter Guards own the park.

In 1922 the Citadel moved to its present location on the Ashley River. However, the old campus has not been forgotten. The Embassy

Suites' façade retains much of the complex's original appearance. There are also two plaques on either side of the hotel's southern entryway. One outlines the history of the site and The Citadel, and the other commemorates the 150th anniversary of the institution's founding. During the military school's years on the site, the property was often referred to as either the Citadel Green or Citadel Square. The latter survives in the name of the nearby Citadel Square Baptist Church.

Beginning in April 2000, the park underwent a $4 million rehabilitation that included the planting of 380 trees, removal of some of the larger, denser shrubs and installation of sandstone benches, bluestone paths and crumbled granite paths. Note the Latin names of trees and continents of origin (e.g. *Magnolia grandiflora — North America*) inscribed in the stones that line the pathways. North of the park, Tobacco Street was cleared of parking and repaved with brick and bluestone treads.

The principal landscape architect and prime consultant for the rehabilitation was Michael Van Valkenburgh Associates Inc. of Cambridge, Mass. Amanda Barton was the city's project manager. The local landscape architect was Wertimer & Associates. The prime contractor was Anson Construction of Ravenel, S.C. The local architect was Studio A Inc. New South Associates of Stone Mountain, Ga. served as archaeology consultant. General Engineering Laboratories Inc. of Charleston provided civil engineering and surveying services. Dulohery, Weeks & Gagliano Inc. of Mount Pleasant, S.C. were the electrical engineers. Ted Rosengarten of McClellanville, S.C., was the cultural consultant. The cost estimator was Costing Services Group Inc. of Atlanta, Ga. John Beardsley of Washington, D.C., and Roberta Sokolitz of Charleston served as art and archival consultants.

Every Saturday, April through December, Marion Square is the site of the Charleston Farmer's Market. The park serves as venue for a number of special events throughout the year: the Southeastern Wildlife Expo (February), the Charleston Food & Wine Festival (March), Piccolo Spoleto (May/June), the MOJA Arts Festival (September/October) and Charleston's Christmas tree lighting ceremony (December).

The Rededication

A rejuvenated Marion Square opened with a rededication ceremony on December 5, 2001. The Citadel Band provided a musical prelude. Mayor Joseph P. Riley Jr. opened the ceremonies by welcoming the several hundred people on hand for the occasion. Captain E.L. Counts, chaplain of the Washington Light Infantry and pastor of St. John's Lutheran Church, provided the invocation.

Members of the Washington Light Infantry and the Sumter Guards made a Presentation of Colors. Chief Rueben Greenberg of the Charleston Police Department led the Pledge of Allegiance. The Citadel Band played the *National Anthem.* In keeping with Marion Square's military tradition, a troop line composed of members of the W.L.I., the Sumter Guards, the Citadel, the South Carolina Army National Guard and the South Carolina State Guard provided an eight-gun artillery salute. Ann Caldwell sang *God Bless America.*

Lieutenant Colonel Dale Theiling's remarks included his enthusiasm for the rejuvenated park: "They have resurrected the Phoenix." Colonel L.C. Fulghum Jr., Marion Square commissioner, said. "The Citadel family looks upon the green as hallowed ground."

Deborah Sisco of the Charleston Rotary Club and Laura Solano of Michael Van Valkenburgh Associates each made brief remarks.

Mayor Riley, Major General H.W. Theiling, Colonel R.B. Scarborough and Colonel L.C. Fulgum Jr. participated in a wreath-laying ceremony.

In his rededication speech, Mayor Riley said, "This is a special event in our city's history. Today, the Green, the Square, has become a public garden, a fine and rich one."

The Rev. Lee Bines, pastor of John Wesley United Methodist Church, concluded the ceremonies with a benediction.

That evening the city's Christmas tree lighting ceremonies took place within the refurbished park.

1. Marion Square Plaque

A bronze plaque highlights some of the extensive history of the park grounds.

In October 1941, the Charleston Historical Commission erected a Belgian block marker to which the plaque was originally affixed. The current marker is composed of sandstone. It is 54 inches high, 38 inches wide and 24 inches deep.

The plaque is attached to the western side of the marker. Scroll-work is at the top. Below are a bas-relief of the city seal and a brief history of the site. At its greatest height, the plaque measures 36 inches; its greatest width is 27½ inches. The United States Bronze Sign Company of New Hyde Park, N.Y. cast the plaque.

2. Hornwork Section

This tiny section of wall is the only reminder of the Herculean efforts and the countless man-hours invested by African-American slaves in the attempt to preserve their masters' freedom. The fragment is a portion of the massive tabby (composed of lime, sand, crushed oyster shell) fortifications erected during the American Revolution to protect the city gates on King Street. Look carefully and you can see the oyster shells. An iron fence encloses the hornwork. There is a small descriptive plaque on the fence.

3. Charleston Rotary Fountain

Six seats invite students, weary visitors and lunchtime loungers to find a moment's respite from the hurly-burly of one of the city's busiest intersections.

The Details

The fountain is high quality pre-cast concrete. The hexagonal-shape mirrors the Rotary seal. Each side is 17 feet, 10 inches in length and contains a seat. The club's traditional "Four-Way Test" — *IS IT FAIR TO ALL CONCERNED? IS IT THE TRUTH? WILL IT BUILD GOOD WILL AND BETTER FRIENDSHIPS? WILL IT BE BENEFICIAL TO ALL CONCERNED?* — is inscribed into the backs of four seats. One of the remaining two seats has the fountain's dedication and the other simply reads: *MARION SQUARE*.

The top basin is a metal bowl with concrete inside. At the center

of the basin is a raised, circular metal fixture with a grate on top. The ring beyond the fixture holds a variety of aquatic plants. Beyond the plants is a circle of metal tubing containing 16 small spouts. The spouts shoot water into an 18-inch circular gutter at the very edge of the top basin from which it sheets down into the lower cobble-lined basin.

There are plans to eventually add art or statuary to the top of the fountain.

The History

As part of the city's Marion Square rehabilitation, plans called for the inclusion of a new fountain. At an early public meeting, members of the Charleston Rotary Club expressed an interest in a "good works" project for the park. A fountain seemed to be the ideal fit. The Rotary had a long association with Marion Square, financing or partially financing beautification projects during the 1940s and 1950s. In 1990 a similar effort by the Rotary led to the installation of a fountain in nearby Wragg Mall.

John Meffert was a key Rotarian in the planning phase. Michael Van Valkenburgh Associates Inc. of Cambridge, Mass. designed the fountain. R.J. Van Seters Company Ltd. of Unionville, Ontario was fountain consultant. Wesco Fountains Inc. of North Venice, Fla., performed the mechanical-electrical work. Anson Construction of Ravenel, S.C., installed the fountain.

The Rotary financed $100,000 of the estimated $275,000 cost.

4. Calhoun Monument

A stone base atop the capital of the high, banded column provides John C. Calhoun's stage. His grim face gazes down. His massive cape flows around him. His right hand rests on his hip, while his left hand clutches a document, in all likelihood the Constitution. Although the statue is made of bronze, it is clear why contemporaries called this imposing individual the "Cast-Iron Man."

The History

The movement to memorialize John C. Calhoun, distinguished and controversial South Carolina statesman, began January 23, 1854, when Amarintha Yates invited 11 ladies to her mother's drawing room to form the Ladies Calhoun Monument Association. On June 28, 1858 — Carolina Day — the cornerstone was laid.

The Yankee Invasion interrupted the project, but eventually the association gave a $44,000 commission to Philadelphia sculptor Albert E. Harnisch. On April 26, 1887, (the 37th anniversary of Calhoun's interment), the monument was unveiled. At the dedication, attended by an estimated 20,000 people, Mayor William A. Courtenay somewhat misread the monument's future, describing it as: "The enduring bronze that is uncovered here, and will here remain a witness to coming generations . . ."

In fact, the ladies of the association were described as aghast. In the first place, the overall casting displayed poor workmanship in several different ways. The great orator seemed to be supporting himself by leaning on a chair. The right index finger pointed in an odd direction, giving it a deformed look. There was also a fashion *faux pas:* Calhoun was wearing a Prince Albert coat, not in style during his lifetime. Finally, instead of four allegorical female figures representing Truth, Justice, the Constitution and History, there was only a single classically clad female, sitting at the Great Nullifier's feet.

An 1895 editorial in The News and Courier offered: "It has been suggested that it (Calhoun's statue) be saved up until the death of the sculptor and then placed over his grave. This plan, however, has been abandoned, the punishment being thought too severe."

On October 31, 1895 (Halloween!), workmen removed the monument from its base. Its fate is unknown, and the only surviving artifact is the infamous index finger, owned by the Charleston Museum.

And so, it was back to the drawing board for The Ladies Calhoun

Monument Association. In 1896 John Massey Rhind (1860-1936) of New York was given a commission of $20,000 to design the second rendition. The official name of the second monument is "Shaft to John C. Calhoun," but the newspapers of the time referred to it as "Mr. Calhoun No. 2."

The Charleston Evening Post reported in the June 27, 1896, edition:

"The Calhoun statue was successfully raised this morning about 9 o'clock to the top of the pedestal and is now in a permanent position.

"The work of elevating the heavy piece of bronze was watched by a large crowd.

"It was done without the slightest hitch.

"The statue appears splendidly."

On July 18, 1898 the Ladies Calhoun Monument Association disbanded, turning perpetual care of the monument over to the city.

During Marion Square's major rehabilitation, Conservation Solutions of District Heights, Md., completed a $101,000 face lift of the monument. The work included a thorough cleaning of all monument elements, repair and repointing of the stone, and after a uniform patination of the bronze, application of a protective coating.

The Details

Only the lowest portion of the pedestal, where the raised *CALHOUN* can be seen, was salvaged from the original monument. The upper pedestal, column, statue and all bronze elements are the creations of John Massey Rhind. The overall height of the monument is described as a towering 80 feet, the statue itself as 15 feet ("A Guide to Confederate Monuments in South Carolina").

A short granite wall, 39 inches from the base, encloses the monument, creating a "moat" with slanted bluestone covering the bottom. The top of the wall has filled holes, providing evidence of an earlier fence that once surrounded the base. The base, measured at its lowest lip, is approximately 34 feet x 34 feet.

The southern face of the pedestal's lower portion features, in large raised and polished lettering, *CALHOUN.*

Four steps lead from the lower tier to the pedestal's upper tier. The four corners of this tier are decorated with 4-foot bronze palmettos.

The southern face of the upper tier bears a wreath, Calhoun's birth and death years, and *Truth, Justice, the Constitution and His-*

tory. All bronze.

There are two bronze bas-reliefs on the higher tier. The eastern one, *Replying to Webster 26 Feb. 1833*, depicts Calhoun in a debate during the Nullification Crisis. Under the lip of the lower right hand corner of the bas-relief is an inscription—*J. Massey Rhind New York.* There is also one more word that begins with "sc"; it might mean sculpted or sculptor, or possibly even Scotsman, which Rhind was. (The fact that I know this detail does not discredit my earlier claim that, "I have not scaled the Calhoun Monument . . ." I did not scale the monument, but "somebody" did partially scale it for me.)

The western bas-relief depicts *Calhoun Reorganizing War Department*. A further inscription reads: *Presented by Sarah Calhoun Simonds,* Calhoun's grandniece. The northern side of the pedestal's upper tier holds a large bronze relief plaque detailing some of the trials and tribulations involved in getting the monuments built.

In his lifetime, Calhoun was at the center of many a political storm. Today, due to the monument's height, his statue is literally a lightning rod during Lowcountry thunderstorms. Note the lightning protection system on the northern side.

The Biography

John Caldwell Calhoun (1782-1850) was born in Abbeville District, S.C., the third son of Patrick, upcountry planter and legislator, and Martha Caldwell Calhoun. His father and sister Catherine died when he was 13, and his mother died when he was 19. Calhoun's widowed brother-in-law, Dr. Moses Waddell, a clergyman, oversaw his early education. Following his father's death, Calhoun worked four years on the home plantation. He then convinced his older brothers, William and James, to finance his college education. Dr. Waddell prepared him for his academic life. He was admitted to Yale as a junior and graduated two years later in 1802.

Calhoun studied law for the next three years in both South Carolina and Connecticut, gaining admission to the South Carolina Bar in 1807.

Calhoun served two terms in the S.C. General Assembly. In November 1810 he was elected to the U.S. House of Representatives. In January 1811 Calhoun married his wealthy second cousin Floride Bonneau Colhoun, with whom he had 10 children, seven surviving to adulthood. Although the couple married for love, his wife's inheritance allowed Calhoun the luxury of ending his legal practice and commencing a life devoted to politics and public service.

As a young congressman, Calhoun joined the "War Hawks," a group made up of mostly Southerners and Westerners in Congress who fervently supported a second war with Great Britain. In 1812, despite his lack of seniority, he was placed in the number two spot on the Foreign Relations Committee. This committee, with the support of President Madison, drafted the declaration of war. At this early stage in his career, Calhoun was a strong nationalist and stalwart supporter of what became an increasingly unpopular war.

In 1817 President Monroe appointed Calhoun as Secretary of War, a position he held for eight years. Many of his efforts to make the American Army more modern, professional and efficient were undercut by a parsimonious Congress. His greatest achievement was transforming West Point (the U.S. Military Academy) from a second-rate outpost into a first-rate military college. His most difficult task was attempting to manage the country's great military hero General Andrew Jackson, particularly during the campaigns in Florida.

Calhoun sought the presidency in the turbulent campaign of 1824, but eventually settled for the vice presidency. Both the John Quincy Adams and Jackson camps nominated him. This oddity occurred due to the temporary demise of the two-party system during the Monroe administration, the so-called "Era of Good Feelings." Calhoun won

the vice presidency, but in the tightly contested presidential election, with a field of four, no candidate received a majority of the electoral votes, so the contest was sent to the House of Representatives for resolution. The House eventually decided the matter in favor of Adams, denying Andrew Jackson his first shot at the presidency.

Calhoun soon broke ranks with Adams over the appointment of Henry Clay as Secretary of State, which many saw as proof of a "corrupt bargain" between the two men. In his capacity as presiding officer of the Senate, Calhoun foiled many of Adams' initiatives, becoming an openly pro-Jackson leader within the administration.

In 1828 Jackson rewarded Calhoun's support by naming him the Democratic vice presidential candidate.

At this time, rifts were beginning to develop between the manufacturing North and the agrarian South, largely due to the divisive issue of tariffs. The Tariff of 1824 raised duties significantly, but proved a double whammy for Southerners due to the plunging prices of cotton. When Adams signed into law the Tariff of 1828, the "Tariff of Abominations," duties were increased an additional 20 percent.

Calhoun was convinced that an oppressive federal government was benefiting Northerners by victimizing Southerners in general and South Carolinians in particular. Calhoun ruminated on a solution to the problem of protecting the minority from tyranny by the majority, and in November 1828 anonymously issued his treatise on what would come to be known as "nullification."

Calhoun theorized that, since the federal government had only been given a few specified powers, all other powers were retained by the individual states. He also did not look upon the ratification of the U.S. Constitution as making the federal government sovereign. He felt the individual states retained their sovereignty and thus the right to determine whether a federal law infringed on the compact that created the Union. If it did, the individual states had the power to declare any such law null and void. Subsequently, if three-quarters of the states upheld the law, the offended state still had the option of either acquiescence or secession.

It was a dangerous stance for a sitting vice president, particularly one about to be overwhelmingly re-elected with Jackson's November victory. By this time Calhoun had started down the road to sectionalism. South Carolina wholeheartedly supported her favorite son. Calhoun's hope was that Jackson's belief in states rights would lead the president to remain neutral in the national debate over the tariffs and, given his new-found power, prompt him to move swiftly to reduce the tariff and avoid the approaching confrontation.

However, events outside the realm of politics strained the relationship between Jackson and Calhoun. The "Petticoat Affair" found Calhoun's wife Floride and most of the cabinet members' wives snubbing Peggy Eaton, wife of Secretary of War John Eaton, concerning questions about her "reputation." Furthermore, leaks were made known to Jackson about former Secretary of War Calhoun's actions and reactions during the military campaigns in Florida. It was clear that Calhoun would not be Jackson's running mate in 1832.

In his famous "Fort Hill Address" of August 1831, Calhoun restated his theories but at the same time attempted to quiet fears about South Carolina's future course.

After the overwhelming Jackson/Van Buren victory in the national elections of 1832, events unfolded rapidly. On November 24, 1832, the South Carolina Constitution Convention nullified the Tariffs of 1824 and 1828. Effective February 1, 1833, federal import duties would no longer have been collected at the port of Charleston. On December 12 the S.C. General Assembly elected Calhoun to the U.S. Senate and on December 28 Calhoun resigned the vice presidency. Jackson promised to use force to collect the tariffs. But the crisis peaked and eventually cooled. Although the Senate authorized a Force Act on February 19, 1833, by March 2 a compromise tariff had been passed.

During the 1830s and 1840s the Senate was the focal point for debates on the country's future. Calhoun was a member of the "Great Triumvirate" that included Henry Clay and Daniel Webster. "The Great Nullifier" became the chief architect and spokesman for states rights as well as the South's greatest defender of slavery.

Calhoun decided to have another go at the presidency in the national elections of 1844. In anticipation of this time-consuming process, he resigned his Senate seat in 1843. However, after testing the political waters thoroughly, he withdrew his candidacy in January 1844 and retired to his home plantation Fort Hill. His retirement was brief.

On February 28, 1844, a huge gun aboard the battleship *Princeton* exploded, killing several dignitaries, including Secretary of State Abel Upshur. President John Tyler called upon Calhoun to fill the vacancy. Less than two weeks after taking office, Calhoun was able to achieve a long-sought-after goal by bringing Texas into the Union as a territory.

By the fall of 1845 the S.C. Legislature returned Calhoun to the Senate.

Although Secretary of State Calhoun's attempts to negotiate a settlement with the British over the Oregon Territory failed, Senator Calhoun continued to pursue a peaceful solution. His March 16, 1846 Senate speech was reasoned and conciliatory, and within roughly three months the Senate ratified a treaty setting the boundary between British Canada and the United States at the 49th parallel, not "Fifty-four forty, or fight!," the slogan of expansionist Democrats in the 1844 presidential campaign.

When the United States declared war on Mexico, Calhoun opposed the conflict. However, when American victory became certain, he opposed the Wilmot Proviso that would have prevented slavery from being extended into the lands acquired from Mexico.

As his health failed in late 1849 and early 1850, Calhoun spent his final energy committing to paper his thoughts on government and its relationship to the governed. If there had ever been any doubt, Calhoun's two posthumous treatises, "Disquisition on Government" and "Discourse on the Constitution and Government of the United States," soon demonstrated his formidable intellect and grasp of the nuances of law and government.

"The Defender of the Constitution" died March 31, 1850, in Washington, D.C. As soon as the telegraph lines brought the sad news to Charleston, the bells of St. Michael's tolled, ships in the harbor lowered their flags and public buildings were draped in black.

After Calhoun was eulogized in the U.S. Senate, his body began the long journey home, transported at various times by steamer, railroad and horse-drawn hearse. In Charleston the funeral procession took two hours to pass any given point along the route.

Although Calhoun would have preferred to be buried at his Upstate plantation, his interment became involved in the politics of the day and his funeral was handled as a matter of state. His tomb is in the St. Philip's Episcopal Church west cemetery.

The Trivia

Calhoun's resignation came December 28, 1832. It was a bit anticlimatic because he had not run as Jackson's vice presidential candidate in the November 1832 election. "Old Hickory" chose Martin Van Buren as his running mate instead. But, in fact, Calhoun could have continued to serve until Inauguration Day — March 4, 1833. He resigned to fill the unexpired term of S.C. Senator Robert Young Hayne, who had just been elected governor.

The only other vice president to resign was Spiro T. Agnew, following the revelation of previous financial improprieties while serving as Baltimore County executive and later as Maryland's governor.

Agnew resigned October 10, 1973, after pleading "no contest" to tax evasion charges. In return, the Justice Department agreed not to pursue bribery charges. He was given three years of unsupervised probation, fined $10,000 and required to pay $150,000 in back taxes.

5. Charleston Holocaust Memorial

The stark, spare memorial intentionally straddles a major pathway running alongside Calhoun Street. Its location and evocative history forces each visitor to confront head-on man's inhumanity toward his fellow man.

The Details

The memorial is described as 6,000 square feet in area (August 17, 1998—The Post and Courier), making it by far the largest monument in the city's parks. Its most striking feature is the 17-foot-tall, mill-finished stainless-steel latticework. Extending outward from the top edge of the latticework and held in place by small brackets is a thin plate from which nails protrude upward.

The area enclosed by the latticework is called the "sanctuary." The entire platform is 86 feet, 8 inches x 28 feet, 8 inches, but the greater portion is composed of specially mixed and finished concrete stained with rusty hues. In the middle, a 16-foot bronze *tallith*, or prayer shawl, is spread. Adjacent to the enclosure is a rectangular, sunken lawn framed by graded steps and providing an area for either assembly or contemplation.

Three plaques are on the interior wall facing Calhoun Street. The relief lettering on the slanted top of the easternmost plaque describes

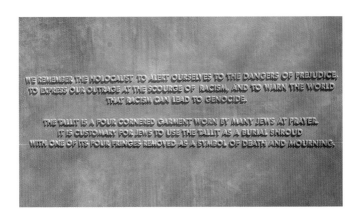

WE REMEMBER THE HOLOCAUST TO ALERT OURSELVES TO THE DANGERS OF PREJUDICE, TO EXPRESS OUR OUTRAGE AT THE SCOURGE OF RACISM, AND TO WARN THE WORLD THAT RACISM CAN LEAD TO GENOCIDE.

THE TALLIT IS A FOUR CORNERED GARMENT WORN BY MANY JEWS AT PRAYER. IT IS CUSTOMARY FOR JEWS TO USE THE TALLIT AS A BURIAL SHROUD WITH ONE OF ITS FOUR FRINGES REMOVED AS A SYMBOL OF DEATH AND MOURNING.

the events of the Holocaust, making clear that the memorial is dedicated to the 11 million people who perished at the hands of the Nazi regime in World War II. An inscription on the plaque's side says:

IN MEMORIAM
TO THOSE WHO PERISHED
IN THE HOLOCAUST
1933-1945

A walkway descends to a second plaque, mounted on the side of the wall. The first words atop the plaque are a biblical quote: "On that day, one who has escaped will come to you, to let you hear it with your own ears." It goes on to list the names of 79 South Carolina Holocaust survivors, their towns and countries of origin. The plaque ends with another biblical quote: "We are a remnant that has survived."

The walkway ascends to a third plaque. The raised lettering on the slanted top describes the collaboration that culminated in the monument's successful completion. An exhortation is made to remember those murdered, honor those who survived and remain vigilant to future atrocities. There is also an explanation of the significance of the *tallith*. In life it is used as a prayer shawl but at death, after the removal of one *tzitzit,* or tassel, it becomes a burial shroud. An inscription on the plaque's side reads:

IN MEMORIAM 1999

Two other plaques, mounted on low stone bases, with relief lettering, can be seen at the eastern and western peripheries of the memorial. The eastern plaque is the cornerstone, honoring the contributors. The western plaque is the dedication, acknowledging those involved

WILLY MORITZ ADLER, HAMBURG, GERMANY
FELIX K. BAUER, VIENNA, AUSTRIA
MARTHA M. BAUER, COLOGNE, GERMANY
LUDWIG BAMBERGER, LICHTENFELS, GERMANY
THEA BAMBERGER, FRANKFURT, GERMANY
GERTRUDE BERNSTEIN, POLAND
WALTER BERNSTEIN, POLAND
RABBI NAPHTALI BERGER, BUDAPEST, HUNGARY
HERSHEL BLASS, LODZ, POLAND
RITA PEPER CURTIN, AMERSFOORT, THE NETHE
ARMAND GEORGES DERFNER, PARIS, FRANCE
RITA DEUTZ-SERPHOS, AMSTERDAM, THE NETH
HELENE DIAMANT, PARIS, FRANCE
MAURICE DIAMANT, MILAN, ITALY
ADOLFO DIAMANTSTEIN, HEIDELBERG, GERMAN
LEO DIAMANTSTEIN, HEIDELBERG, GERMANY
STEPHAN DRUCKER, GERMANY
BEN ENGEL, ZAKROCZYM, POLAND

in the project. Despite the date on the plaque (April 13, 1999), the actual dedication took place June 6, 1999. A nearby drainage problem caused the delay. The original plan was for a May dedication on Yom HaShoah, Holocaust Memorial Day, but D-Day (the Allied invasion of Normandy, France, on June 6, 1944) was a good second choice.

The memorial's construction was only one of the goals of remembrance. Of equal importance, located just down the street at the Charleston County Public Library at 68 Calhoun Street, are the Jerry and Anita Zucker Holocaust Memorial Collection and Archives. There students and the general public may enhance their knowledge of the Holocaust with audio/visual testimonies, manuscripts and artifacts of both survivors and their liberators.

The History

The Charleston Holocaust Memorial is the dream of Holocaust survivor and retired King Street merchant Joe Engel. One day in 1994 over breakfast, he wondered aloud to friends Pincus Kolender and Charles Markowitz why Charleston didn't have a Holocaust memorial. Engel took the initiative and wrote a letter to Mayor Joseph P. Riley Jr. The mayor responded positively to the idea, and the three survivors, with the help of Charleston architect Jeffrey Rosenblum, rallied the Jewish community.

Under the aegis of the Charleston Jewish Federation, a Holocaust Memorial Committee was formed. A Marion Square location was proposed and the Washington Light Infantry and Sumter Guards donated the site.

The Committee advertised nationally for design proposals. From among the 15 received, a joint venture planned by Jonathan Levi Architects Inc. (formerly Stein/Levi Architects Inc.) of Boston and Design Works, a Charleston landscape architecture and urban design firm, was selected.

In April 1997 the Mayor's Design Review Committee recommended the plans, Mayor Riley endorsed them and the City of Charleston's Board of Architectural Review gave its final approval. A ground-breaking ceremony took place July 23 and construction began several weeks later.

At the same time, more than $450,000 was raised from approximately 600 private and corporate donors.

In addition to Jonathan Levi Architects Inc. and Design Works, Parks Director Steve Livingston and Preservation Officer Charles Chase were important members of the design team. The contractor was Stier, Kent & Canady Inc. of Charleston. Jonathan Levi was both the memorial's architect and sculptor of the *tallith*.

The Dedication

On June 6, 1999, approximately 2,000 people gathered at 7 p.m. for the hour-long dedication. Accepting the memorial on behalf of the city, Mayor Riley said, "This is Charleston's gift to the efforts of the human race to make sure we never, ever forget." Holocaust Committee Chair David Popowski echoed the mayor's sentiment: "May all who see it absorb its message so history will never again record an act such as the Holocaust."

While the Charleston Symphony Orchestra played music from the motion picture "Schindler's List," Jennifer Henriques Phillips, development chair, read the names of 79 Holocaust survivors living in South Carolina. Anita Zucker, fund-raising chair, read a letter of congratulations from S.C. Governor Jim Hodges.

Also taking part in the dedication were the Very Reverend William N. McKeachie, dean of the Cathedral Church of St. Luke and St. Paul and president of the Christian-Jewish Council of Charleston; architect Jeffrey Rosenblum, design chair; Rabbi Anthony D. Holz of Kahal Kadosh Beth Elohim; Rabbi David J. Radinsky of Brith Sholom Beth Israel; and Rabbi Edward M. Friedman of Synagogue Emanu-El, president of the Greater Charleston Clergy Association.

D'Jaris Whipper Lewis sang *the Star Spangled Banner"* and Sarah C. Yablon sang the Israeli national anthem.

6. Cast Iron Fountain

The charming old fountain is the park's most soothing feature.

The Details

Water jets two feet before falling into the upper basin and trickling down through "leaves" to the pool below. Both the base of the tapered fountain pedestal and the lower basin are octagonal. There are a number of botanical designs in the pedestal and both basins. Small, inverted *fleurs-de-lis* can be seen in the pedestal. Larger, more stylized *fleurs-de-lis* can be seen on the underside of the top basin, while smaller flowers decorate the exterior of the lower basin. Each side is 6 feet, 8 inches in length. The lower basin is 2-feet-4 inches deep.

The History

The fountain appears to be circa 1880s. A "sister" fountain also owned by the city was recovered from the courtyard of the Food Court at Church and South Market streets prior to the building's razing. It was later installed in the tiny park at Elizabeth, John and Chapel streets.

In February 2007, B&B Services of Moncks Corner sandblasted the Marion Square fountain. It was primed and a fresh coat of green paint was applied.

7. Hampton Obelisk

Obelisks should be impressive. This one is not. Wade Hampton deserves better.

The Details

The official name of the obelisk is Memorial to Wade Hampton, a prominent 19th century Confederate general and South Carolina politician. Five slightly irregularly shaped granite squares of decreasing size — 9 feet, 9 inches x 9 feet, 8 inches; 8 feet, 6 inches x 8 feet, 7 inches; 6 feet, 8 inches x 6 feet, 8 ½ inches; 5 feet, x 5 feet; and 3 feet, 6 inches x 3 feet, 6 inches—form the base of the obelisk, described as 25 feet in height (March 28,1912—The News and Courier).

The four faces of the top two bases contain historic details. The inscriptions on the western face give credit to the Charleston Chapter, United Daughters of the Confederacy, although the correct dedication year is 1912, not 1911. The southern inscriptions provide Hampton's years of tenure as South Carolina governor and U.S. senator. The eastern face has raised and originally polished lettering featuring his name and the years of his life span. The inscriptions in the northern face chronicle his military career.

The Biography

Wade Hampton III (1818-1902) was born in the Colonel William Rhett House at 54 Hasell Street, Charleston. It was the home of his maternal grandfather, Christopher FitzSimons. His parents were Wade Hampton II and Ann FitzSimons Hampton.

Hampton was raised at Millwood, a family estate near Columbia. He graduated from South Carolina College in 1836, the same year he married Margaret Preston. They had four children before Margaret's death in 1852. Hampton married Mary Singleton McDuffie in 1858. The couple also had four children.

Hampton was trained as a lawyer but largely used his legal skills as a legislator, serving in both the South Carolina House and Senate before the War for Southern Independence. He also managed the family's extensive land holdings in Louisiana, Mississippi, North Carolina and South Carolina.

With war's approach, the governor commissioned Hampton as a colonel and allowed him to raise volunteers for his own command. He quickly organized and financed "Hampton's Legion," a unit consisting of companies of infantry, cavalry and artillery. Although having no previous military experience, he became an excellent commander. His infantry company was involved in the war's first great battle at Manassas, Va. Under his direct command, his unit blocked a Union flanking maneuver at the Battle of First Manassas (First Bull Run). He was wounded in the fighting.

Hampton became a brigadier general in June 1862 and soon afterward was wounded again at the Battle of Seven Pines, Va. He received his first cavalry command in July 1862, serving under General James Ewell Brown Stuart. In September 1862, he fought in the Antietam, Va., campaign and later led a series of successful raids during the winter of 1862-63.

On July 3, 1863, during the Battle of Gettysburg, Pa., Hampton received two saber wounds. During his convalescence, he was commissioned as a major general. Several months after Stuart's death in May 1864, Hampton assumed command of General Robert E. Lee's cavalry of the Confederate Army of Northern Virginia.

Hampton's men distinguished themselves in the fall of 1864 through a series of actions that kept communication lines open between Richmond and areas south and west of the city. However, the single act that won Hampton the greatest acclaim from his fellow soldiers was the capture of 2,486 head of Yankee cattle. For several weeks, Lee's hungry troops dined on "Hampton Steaks."

In January 1865, faced with a critical shortage of horses, Hampton and part of his command left Virginia and headed to South Carolina to acquire new mounts. He was promoted to lieutenant general in February and shortly thereafter, attempted to screen General Joseph Johnston's retreat through the Carolinas. With the approach of General William T. Sherman's Union forces, Hampton and his men were forced to abandon the state capital, Columbia. At the war's end, although Hampton wished to continue guerilla warfare rather than accept defeat, he did sign a parole and headed home.

Although Hampton suffered great property losses during the war, including his beloved Millwood, his greatest losses were the deaths of his brother Frank and his son Preston.

Despite his initial reluctance to accept defeat, he supported U.S. President Andrew Johnson's call for reunion. Urged to run for the governorship in 1865, he declined, feeling his earlier advocacy of continued resistance might have made him a target for Northern criticism.

After chairing the state Democratic Executive Committee during the presidential campaign of 1868, Hampton withdrew from politics and moved to Mississippi, after which his indebtedness forced him into bankruptcy. He retained only a modest home in Columbia and the smallest of his Mississippi plantations, *Wild Woods*. In 1869 Hampton joined the Southern Life Insurance Company as an executive, managing the Baltimore branch. He returned frequently

to his home state, where many whites chafed under the rule of the Republicans. He spoke before a crowd of 6,000 at the June 16, 1870, dedication of the Washington Light Infantry's monument at Magnolia Cemetery. Due to his wife's ill health, he returned home to Columbia, where she died in March 1874.

By early 1876 only South Carolina, Louisiana and Florida remained under Republican reconstruction control. Many white South Carolinians thought the time was right to reclaim control of the state. Many thought Wade Hampton was the man to lead this resurgence. Hampton made his intentions clear by participating in the centennial celebration of the Battle of Sullivan's Island in Charleston. By August the Democrats had nominated a full slate of office seekers, with Hampton leading the ticket as gubernatorial candidate. The year 1876 saw turbulent elections at both national and state levels. Hampton became governor by a narrow margin in an election marred by intimidation, terror and violence against black voters and politicians, as the white Democrats "redeemed" their state.

Despite cries of foul play and calls for new elections, Hampton was inaugurated December 13, 1876. He was in Washington in late March 1877 and upon his return to South Carolina, he came bearing the blessings of President Rutherford B. Hayes and a promise for the removal of federal occupation troops.

Soon after his re-election in 1878, Hampton broke his right leg in a hunting accident. Eventually the leg was amputated. In early 1879 he resigned the governorship when the General Assembly elected him to the U.S. Senate. South Carolina had a unique senatorial tandem. Senator Matthew C. Butler was a war amputee.

Hampton became a conservative and largely moderating force in South Carolina. A former slave owner, his attitude toward blacks was paternalistic, and although he did not believe in racial equality, he did believe in fair play. In general, he protected the hard-won rights of African Americans. Eventually though, a more radical and racist wing of the Democratic Party emerged in the state. Edgefield's Benjamin "Pitchfork Ben" Tillman, who won the governorship in 1890, personified this new attitude. After Tillman swept into power, Hampton relinquished his Senate seat in early 1891.

In 1892 President Grover Cleveland appointed Hampton as U.S. Railroad Commissioner, a position he held until 1897.

Hampton's last public appearance was at South Carolina College's alumni reunion in December 1901. He caught a cold and its effects along with existing heart disease significantly weakened him. He died April 11, 1902, at home in Columbia. Two days later, Bishop Ellison Capers, a friend and fellow Confederate general, conducted his funeral. (See Ellison Capers Tablet—Washington Square.)

The Dedication

The Charleston Chapter, United Daughters of the Confederacy, dedicated the monument on March 28, 1912, the 94th anniversary of Hampton's birth. The dedication was the culmination of eight years of work, which raised roughly $2,000.

However, the monument was not an easy sell. City Council did not consider it grand enough for White Point Garden. Amazingly, the park commissioners even rejected its placement in Hampton Park in uptown Charleston! Finally, the Marion Square Commissioners provided space on the park's east side.

A large audience, including many military companies and cadets from Porter Military Academy and the Citadel attended the ceremonies. Colonel James Simons presided. The Right Rev. William A. Guerry, bishop of South Carolina, delivered the invocation. Corinne and Eloise Hampton (granddaughters), Sally Hampton Lindsey (great-granddaughter) and Gertrude and Lucy Hampton (grandnieces) completed the unveiling. Mrs. Randolph Tucker and

McDuffie Hampton (two of Hampton's children) were also on hand.

The Metz and the Citadel Cadet bands provided the music, including *Dixie.* The German Artillery fired a salute. A number of wreaths were laid upon the monument's base. One bore an original poem titled "Hampton," penned by the Rev. Dr. P.L. Duffy, chaplain of the Irish Volunteers. Soon after the wreath-laying, it began to rain and the ceremonies were moved to the nearby Citadel chapel.

After some selections by the two bands, Simons expressed his regrets about the weather and made a brief tribute to Hampton. He next presented Dr. S.C. Mitchell, orator for the occasion and president of the University of South Carolina. Mitchell commented on the memorial's proximity to the Calhoun monument and the Citadel campus. He extolled Hampton, likening him to George Washington and Robert E. Lee, other great American warriors who made equal contributions in peacetime. At the end of his address, Mitchell said, "The achievements of Hampton may mean less and less as the generations pass but the character of Hampton will stand out more and more clearly in its essential attributes to the posterity of the people of the State for all time to come."

Bishop Guerry closed the exercises with the benediction.

Waterfront Park

A calm, quiet setting, open spaces and beautiful views are only a few reasons to love Waterfront Park.

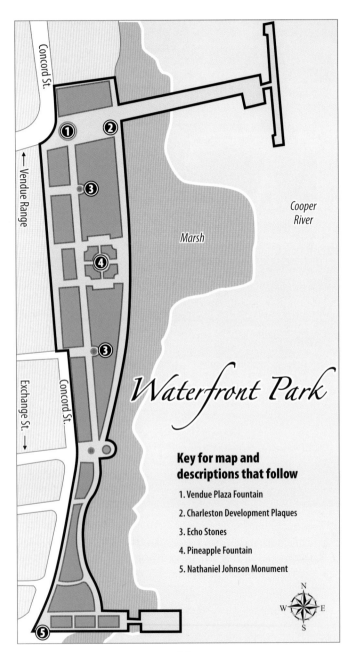

Concord St.

← Vendue Range

① ②

③

Cooper
River

Marsh

④

③

Exchange St. →

Concord St.

Waterfront Park

Key for map and descriptions that follow

1. Vendue Plaza Fountain

2. Charleston Development Plaques

3. Echo Stones

4. Pineapple Fountain

5. Nathaniel Johnson Monument

⑤

N
W   E
S

The Location

Dedicated May 11, 1990, Waterfront Park is the newest major park in Charleston. The approximately 12-acre tract stretches from the restored and supplemented saltwater marshes beyond the park's walls along the Cooper River inland to Concord Street. Its southern terminus is North Adger's Wharf and its northern terminus is Vendue Range. There are entrances off East Bay Street at North Adger's Wharf, Exchange Street, Middle Atlantic Wharf and Vendue Range.

The History

Much of the land that comprises the park today was once a busy shipping site. However, after the War of Secession, shipping patterns began to change and the port moved northward. The earthquake of 1886 further accelerated decline. In 1955 a fire destroyed the wharves and buildings of the Clyde Steamship Lines, and the area did not recover. By the 1970s the dominant features were rotting piles, parking lots and under utilized warehouses.

The park's origins date back to February 1976 when Charles and Elizabeth Woodward gave the city a donation to pay for the reconstruction of North Adger's Wharf, an early commercial dock dating to the late 17th century. Soon afterward, plans for a private development of the waterfront site surfaced. To protect this important resource, the city purchased the land in 1979. The acquisition led Mayor Joseph P. Riley Jr. to begin efforts to clean up the entire Cooper River waterfront by building a park and encouraging private redevelopment on adjacent sites.

In 1979 the city interviewed firms to develop a master plan for the peninsula, including a waterfront park. Sasaki Associates of Watertown, Mass., was chosen to lead the project. Mayor Riley added Ed Pinckney Associates of Hilton Head Island and architect Jacquelin T. Robertson of New York to the team. Sasaki's Stuart O. Dawson was the primary designer.

Working drawings were prepared in the mid-1980s. Phase I of construction, stabilizing and strengthening the soils and reconstructing North Adger's Wharf began with a groundbreaking ceremony on August 16, 1983, the 200th anniversary of the city's incorporation.

On February 4, 1985 a rededication of North Adger's Wharf took place, officially marking the end of Phase I. Despite the raw weather, about 75 people attended the ceremonies. As a concession to the cold,

Mayor Riley cut his speech short but announced the kickoff of a $3 million fund-raising drive. Capers G. Barr III, fund-raiser chair, broke a ceremonial bottle of champagne on the reconstructed wharf.

On January 23, 1988, a crowd of 250 watched as both Mayor Riley and Senator Strom Thurmond ceremonially drove pilings to begin Phase II. Once work began, City Parks Director Steven Livingston was involved with planning oversight and much of the landscape architecture, and Mario Ciappa, city engineer, managed the project. Ruscon Construction Company of Charleston was the prime contractor.

Work proceeded on schedule, with an anticipated dedication in early May 1990. However, on September 21, 1989, Hurricane Hugo slammed Charleston. Although the park sustained $1 million in damage, most was confined to the trees, plants and ornamental elements. Amazingly, the major structures—the new walls and pier—withstood the brunt of the storm.

The park's total cost was $13.5 million, financed by private donations and grants, tax increment bonds, county funds, community development and revenue-sharing funds, and a $3.3 million Urban Development Action Grant.

The Dedication

Only a week behind schedule, the park was dedicated the evening of May 11, 1990. In an emotional dedication speech, Mayor Riley pronounced the park a gift from the present community that would "touch the souls" of future generations. The Charleston Symphony Orchestra entertained thousands who gathered for the ceremony. Capping the festivities, Riley simultaneously turned on all the park's lights and the two fountains.

At the Vendue Range park entrance, there is a dedication plaque listing Mayor Riley and members of City Council who served through the planning, design and construction stages.

The Details

The park has two wharves. North Adger's Wharf, a reconstructed colonial dock, sits at the southern end, and the new Vendue Wharf is at the northern end. In front of North Adger's Wharf, fenced in on the north and south by 43-inch pillars, with heavy links of chain between them, are three huge planters containing knobby-limbed London plane trees, Asiatic jasmine and seasonal flowers. A 40-foot ramp leads from the gardens to the reconstructed wharf, but more importantly, it transports you back to the colony's earliest commercial days. Invisible beneath the massive blocks of stone are "rafts," strapped-together palmetto logs, a means of spreading the wharf's weight over a large area. Atop the stone base lies a 96-foot-by-44-foot plank deck with plank benches on all except the harbor side.

Approaching the park straight on from Vendue Range, there is a large radial jet fountain, and beyond it a bluestone-paved plaza. The plaza leads to the 365-foot Vendue Wharf, which holds three shade structures, beneath which are large swings and seating. The middle structure features a cupola, dormers and a dolphin weathervane. Near the end of the wharf is a maritime flagpole upon which the blue-and-white state flag is to the left, a higher U.S. flag is in the middle, and the blue-and-white city flag is to the right. At the end of the wharf, at a lower level, is a 280-foot fishing pier that runs parallel to the park over deep water.

At the Vendue Range end of the park and at the Middle Atlantic Wharf entrance are gated entrances. Charleston blacksmith and icon Philip Simmons was a consultant and co-designer of the "Egret Gates." Ornamental railings surround the northern park.

At the park's heart is the spectacular Pineapple Fountain. The "Great Lawn" frames it on either side. Raised and spacious, this wonderful green expanse can accommodate a large number of people involved in a variety of activities. A 1,200-foot palmetto-lined, crushed stone riverside promenade links North Adger's to Vendue Range. Within the park's boundaries are formal gardens, planters, bosques of live oaks, tree-shaded walking paths, seating areas and drinking fountains.

Waterfront Park has received national recognition as well as numerous awards. In 2008 the American Planning Association named the park one of the nation's 10 Great Public Spaces. The list included New York City's Central Park. In 2007 the park won a Landmark Award from the American Society of Landscape Architects and the National Trust for Historic Preservation.

The park's setting affords panoramic views of the bay, including the World War II aircraft carrier *Yorktown,* the Arthur Ravenel Jr. Bridge, Shute's Folly and the remains of Castle Pinckney. In the distance is Fort Sumter. Dolphins, egrets and pelicans are only a few of the animals commonly seen in the restored marshland and beyond.

1. Vendue Plaza Fountain

Your first instinct is to dash under the arcs but common sense should prevail, thus confirming your worst fear—you are no longer a child!

The Details

The grand radial jet fountain has a diameter of just under 50 feet. Sixteen 3-foot polished granite bollards hold bronze jets and lights. The fountain's floor is in the design of an abstract compass, composed of four concentric rings of thermal, slip-proof granite alternating between different "quarry colors" that converge on a central 9-foot diameter raised "splash stone." Above the stone, the arcs of water join to form a cone. The top of the stone is composed of an outer ring of granite, a circular metal plate holding four lights that illuminate the cone at night, and smack-dab in the middle, unseen except during shutdowns, a 34-inch-diameter city seal.

On the park side are two concentric circles that create steps leading up to the circular plaza. From the Vendue Range side, there are seven concentric arcs that form steps leading directly up to the fountain, but only five steps approach from either the left or right.

Stu Dawson of Sasaki Associates headed a team that designed the fountain. The fountain cost approximately $300,000. The intent was for it to be a participatory park feature for older children to play in. Since both park fountains are used in this fashion, the water is filtered, monitored and treated like a swimming pool. The sandwich boards at the park entrances detail state health regulations.

2. Charleston Development Plaques

Sometimes we look at nature and our environment as immutable but a glance at these four maps clearly shows, for better or worse, man's impact.

The four 4-foot-by-4-foot maps feature the Charleston peninsula during the 17th, 18th, 19th and 20th centuries. In addition, each of the maps encapsulates some of the high points of the city's history during that century. At Mayor Riley's request, Adm. Arthur M. Wilcox, retired editor of the News and Courier, wrote the plaques' text. Sasaki Associates' proximity to the Perkins Institute for the Blind in Watertown, Mass., inspired the three-dimensional maps and the Braille translation of the historical surveys.

The most obvious difference in the maps is the transformation of marshland into dry land, principally through land-filling. At some point, the city may erect a 21st century plaque. The changes that plaque might reflect would include the disappearance of the Grace and Pearman Bridges and the appearance of the Arthur Ravenel Jr. Bridge. J & M Foundry of Summerville cast the plaques.

3. Echo Stones

Despite their hard surface these stones are incredibly inviting. Along the tree-shaded walking path are two 11-foot-diameter stones. Sasaki designed these stones and the 8-foot square one near the Middle Atlantic entrance as bases for future additions, such as sculptures, statues or monuments. However, since there was a five-year moratorium on new installations and a provision to limit additions to no more than one every 10 years, it was thought that, in the meantime, the stones could be used for sitting, lounging or picnicking.

It is often said that history has unintended consequences, and so does architecture. An unforeseen feature of the round stones is that, by standing atop them in the back angle of the square and facing the water, you get an echo-chamber effect when you speak. "Echo stone" is not a term coined by Sasaki.

4. The Pineapple Fountain

This magnificent fountain emphatically demonstrates the duality of water, its potential for either destructiveness or tranquility. Water gushes violently through the top leaves of the pineapple crown, cascades through the lower leaves, passes through the troughs between the hexagonal units of the truncated rind, drops into the first basin, flows gently into the second basin and finally trickles into the wading pool.

The Details

The leaves were modeled and cast by the Paul King Foundry of Johnston, R.I. The bronze castings were chemically treated to create the green patina and accelerate the oxidation process. Although the fountain bowls appear to be limestone, they are actually cast stone, a stronger and far more durable alternative. Lazamby Precast of Alabama cast them. Each bowl was cast in three sections and then assembled on site. The fountain is 20 feet in width. It is lighted at night.

The plaza was designed to create a serene setting for enjoying the fountain. The plaza is 60 feet, 6 inches x 60 feet, 6 inches, and enclosed by a cast stone seat wall. There are cutouts at each of the four corners. Just beyond each cutout is a planter 12 feet in diameter holding a palmetto and a bed of seasonal flowers. Four bluestone paths, 5 feet wide on the north and south and 10 feet wide on the east and west, lead into a small central plaza composed of tempered granite pavers that surround the fountain. Three approaches are ramps and the eastern entrance has three steps leading to a ramp. These pathways divide the plaza into quadrants. Each is planted in seasonal flowers with arcs of boxwoods immediately behind the curved, polished granite benches that surround the fountain. The inner plaza has four tempered granite steps leading into the pool.

To assure the heavy fountain's stability on the in-filled land, 60-foot piles were driven prior to construction.

Sasaki Associates' Jeff Faber led a team that designed the fountain. Georgia Fountain Company of Atlanta provided the equipment that was customized to fit the design. The fountain cost approximately $275,000. It was intended for a younger audience to use as a wading pool.

Sasaki's Varoujan Hagopian described the fountain's powerful impact: "It became the crystal chandelier of the park."

The History

The genesis of the selection of a giant, stylized pineapple fountain as the park's centerpiece emerged after Mayor Riley gave the design and planning team a four-hour tour of the city. A recurring theme was the extensive use of the pineapple as a decorative element. The pineapple represents hospitality, an appropriate symbol for the city that is annually recognized as the nation's *número uno* in that particular category. This legacy, however, is a time-honored one.

On January 9, 1861, in the run-up to the War of the Rebellion, the Union vessel *Star of the West* was attempting to resupply the Federal troops at Fort Sumter when Citadel cadets fired on the ship. An officer on board commented: "The people of Charleston pride themselves on their hospitality, but it exceeded my expectations. They gave us several balls before we landed."

5. Nathaniel Johnson Monument

A rather simple monument belies the complicated and controversial man it honors.

The Details

The 5-foot-2-inch granite monument honoring Proprietary Governor Nathaniel Johnson stands on a small base. The coat of arms of the Society of First Families of South Carolina 1670-1700 is at the top of the marker. Despite the 1984 engraving, the monument was dedicated in 1985. E.J. McCarthy & Sons Monument Co. of Charleston created the marker.

The majority of the inscription describes highlights of Nathaniel Johnson's life. However, several are somewhat misleading. For instance:

HE SECURED PASSAGE OF THE CHURCH ACT OF

1706, ENDING THE SECTARIAN STRIFE WHICH HAD
BEEN SAPPING THE STRENGTH OF THE COLONY BY
MAKING THE ANGLICAN FAITH THE STATE
RELIGION.

There is no mention that Johnson and his supporters instigated the turmoil. Another questionable passage is:

HE FIRST PROMOTED THE CULTURE OF SILK
WHICH BECAME ONE OF THE LEADING EXPORTS OF
COLONIAL SOUTH CAROLINA.

Whether he was the first to promote the silk culture is unclear, but silk never became a significant export. In 1749, for instance, when the total value of Charlestown's exports reached £161,365 sterling, raw silk exports accounted for only £228 sterling. The three major exports — rice, deerskins and indigo — accounted for 87.5 percent of the total. Johnson's plantation was named *Silk Hope*, and that's all the silk culture ever was, a vague hope.

The Biography

Sir Nathaniel Johnson (1644-1712) was born in Kibblesworth, Durham County, England. He was the son of William, former mayor of Newcastle-upon-Tyne, and Margaret Sherwood Johnson. As a young man, he relocated to Barbados, eventually serving as deputy treasurer.

Johnson returned to Newcastle in 1673, where he served on a number of commissions captained the local militia. He was involved in the Baltic trade. He was knighted December 28, 1680.

Johnson served as mayor (1681-82), alderman (1682-88) and Member of Parliament (1680-81, 1685). His political connections won him appointment as governor of the Leeward Islands (St. Christopher, Nevis, Antigua and Montserrat).

In 1686 Johnson returned to the Caribbean and began to acquire extensive land grants in Carolina. His administration oversaw the strengthening of the islands' defenses, the fostering of improved relations with the Catholic population of the former French colony Montserrat and a general overhauling of the existing legal and court systems. In April 1689, learning of William of Orange's invasion of England and James II's flight into exile, Johnson prepared to leave his post and move to Carolina. He hoped to avoid pledging his allegiance to the new monarchs William and Mary. However, there were nasty but unsubstantiated rumors that his resignation and departure were necessitated due to his role in a plot to turn the islands over to the French to gain support for his deposed king.

As Johnson prepared to begin a new life in Carolina, he sent his wife, Joanna, and their three children home to England only to have them captured and imprisoned by the French. His wife died in captivity but eventually Johnson won his children's release.

From 1689 to 1702 Johnson lived the life of a private citizen in South Carolina, developing his holdings as well as his political contacts. His pride and joy was his plantation on the Cooper River, *Silk Hope.* There he conducted botanical experiments, including, as the name suggests, trying to unravel the mysteries of the silk culture. But *Silk Hope's* major crop was rice.

Johnson became leader of the Goose Creek Men, named for the area north of Charles Towne where many of them resided. This political alliance was strongly Anglican and opposed both the Dissenter (non-Anglican) majority in the colonial legislature and the colony's owners, the Lords Proprietors. In 1700 the Goose Creek Men wrested control of the Governor's Council (the upper house of the colonial legislature) from the Dissenters. In June 1702 through the influence of Sir John Granville, chairman of the proprietary board and a strong Anglican, Johnson was appointed governor. Illness prevented him from immediately assuming the reins of power. In 1703, after recovering, Johnson began to consolidate the power of the Anglicans. The Commons House of Assembly was due to convene May 10. He called for a special session on April 26 but somehow neglected to notify the Dissenters. By a single vote, the Exclusion Act passed, allowing only Anglicans to serve in the legislature. Later in the year, the Establishment Act was passed, making the Church of England the province's official church. These acts created turmoil in South Carolina, where religious tolerance had always made the colony attractive to those of many faiths.

Johnson's opponents on both sides of the ocean successfully prevailed upon the House of Lords, the Privy Council and Queen Anne to overturn the laws. Despite this setback, by 1706 he and his allies managed to push through a watered-down version of the Establishment Act. The new legislation divided the province into 10 Anglican parishes, each supported by tax levies upon all the people, not just members of the Church of England.

Perhaps Johnson's greatest achievement during his tenure was the city's fortification. Just as he had done in the Caribbean, he pushed the colonial assembly to appropriate the necessary funds to shore up Charles Towne's defenses. Colonel William Rhett, the future "Scourge of the Pirates," was appointed to oversee construction. In early 1704 the huge public works project began, employing countless carpenters, bricklayers and slave laborers. Johnson's precautions were soon vindicated.

In 1706 during Queen Anne's War, a French and Spanish invasion force threatened the city. On August 28 a messenger under a flag of truce informed Johnson that he had an hour to surrender before hostilities began. He rebuffed the offer, stating he needed less than a minute's time to refuse.

Two days later Spanish troops landed just north of the city where militiamen soundly defeated them. The next day the versatile Rhett, with a force of armed sloops and brigantines, sailed down the Cooper River to confront the French ships. Bad weather prevented an engagement, but the French left the harbor. Several more French and Spanish raiding parties attacked both north and south of the city but to no avail.

The fortifications were only part of the reason for the colony's success. Equally important were Johnson's leadership and military skills and the combativeness of the colony's militia. Although the French and Spanish forces didn't realize it, not all the fortifications were complete. However, this close call was sufficient to stimulate additional efforts to finish the walls.

Lord Granville's death in 1706 began Johnson's political decline. By 1709 the Lords Proprietors replaced him with Edward Tynte, who restored order in the restive colony. Johnson lived out the remainder of his life at Silk Hope.

The Dedication

On April 27, 1985, the Society of First Families held its General Assembly at the Carolina Yacht Club at 50 East Bay Street. After the election of officers, the membership proceeded to North Adger's Wharf for the dedication and unveiling.

The Trivia

Robert Johnson (circa1676-1735), son of Sir Nathaniel Johnson, followed in his father's footsteps, serving twice as governor. He was the last proprietary governor (1717-1719) and later served as royal governor (1730-1735).

Washington Square

W ashington Square is a 1.48-acre park bound by Meeting, Chalmers and Broad streets, and on the east by the Daniel Ravenel House at 68 Broad Street and the German Friendly Society at 29 Chalmers Street.

The History

The rehabilitation of the area that now comprises Washington Square began with the Great Fire of 1796 that swept through the area, destroying the Old Beef Market at the northeastern corner of

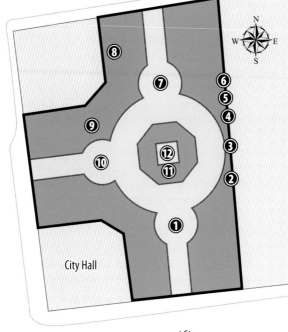

Washington Square

Chalmers St.

Meeting St.

City Hall

Broad St.

Key for map and descriptions that follow

1. Timrod Art Memorial
2. Francis Salvador Plaque
3. Beauregard Memorial Arch
4. John Christie Plaque
5. Ellison Capers Tablet
6. Governor Robert Gibbes Plaque
7. Elizabeth Jackson Monument
8. The Dancing Children
9. Washington Memorial Tree Marker
10. George Washington Statue
11. Centennial Time Capsule
12. Washington Light Infantry Monument

Broad and Meeting streets. The park began as part of the City Square following the completion of the First Bank of the United States building at 80 Broad Street in 1801. In 1818 the bank building became Charleston City Hall.

The park was developed in its present form during the administration of Mayor William Ashmead Courtenay (1879-1887). Originally named City Hall Park, it was renamed Washington Square on October 19, 1881, the centennial of the American-French victory over the British at the Battle of Yorktown. On October 20, 1881, the following announcement appeared in The News and Courier:

"The old City Park passed out of date yesterday one hundred years after the surrender of Cornwallis. It is henceforth to be known as Washington Square, and it is not improbable that a statue of the Father of his Country will soon occupy a conspicuous place within the enclosure."

(Would I not be incorrect in citing the foregoing phrase as an example of the double negative?)

As you'll soon see, the newspaper's prediction was wishful thinking. Since 1881 it has been named Washington Square. Well, except for a few days back in June 2007 when a sign temporarily renamed it STEVEN WASHINGTON PARK! As it turns out the city was preparing to rename Honey Hill Park on Fort Johnson Road on James Island for the long-time baseball coach of the James Island Pirates, but inadvertently the sign was erected in the square instead. It spent the weekend there before being quietly whisked away. Ah, but there was a second oops! Coach Washington's first name is spelled S-T-E-P-H-E-N. However, on June 30, 2007, when the ball field was dedicated with Mr. Washington in attendance, the spelling error was corrected.

In 2000 Theodore F. Monnich of Columbia, S.C., completed thorough cleanings of the "Dancing Children" and the Timrod and Jackson memorials. The bronze elements required the removal of copper oxide, algae and lichens stains as well as ever-troublesome *guano*, or bird poop, prior to the application of a protective coating.

Between 2003 and 2006 the park's fences and walls were restored, repaired or replaced. Glenn Keyes Architects of Charleston and the American College of the Building Arts Inc. planned the project. The city provided the materials and the work was done by building-arts students of ACBA, Clemson University and the College of Charleston, under the supervision of Simeon Warren, dean of ACBA.

The Trivia

The Fireproof Building (1822), home of the South Carolina Historical Society, stands at the northwestern corner of the public square. Charlestonian Robert Mills designed the structure and in 1836 was appointed U.S. Architect by President Andrew Jackson. He designed the Treasury Building, the Patent Office and the General Post Office in Washington, D.C. In 1838 he won the Washington National Monument Society's competition. Simply put, he designed the Washington Monument.

1. Timrod Art Memorial

The bust of a handsome young man with haunting eyes gazes off in a southerly direction.

The Details

The bust of 19th century poet Henry Timrod is the work of Edward Virginius Valentine (1838-1930) of Richmond, Va. His selection was not a surprise. The city had earlier commissioned Valentine to sculpt a marble bust of Mayor William A. Courtenay, which is displayed in the nearby City Council Chamber.

On the Timrod bust, note "Edward V. Valentine Sculptor 1901" is inscribed on a diagonal on the right shoulder. The H.J. Hardenburg Company of New York designed the pedestal. Note at the bottom of the right shoulder "Henry-Bonnard Bronze Co. Founders N.Y. 1901." This company cast the bust and plaques. It was also the founder of the Washington Light Infantry monument's bronzework.

The stonework was completed in the Charleston yards of Thomas H. Reynolds. The southern plaque bears Timrod's name, birth date and birthplace, and the date and place of his death. The year of Timrod's birth is incorrect but the fact that he was born in 1828 was not discovered until 1935. Inscribed in the pedestal below the plaque is the year 1901, when it was dedicated.

The eastern plaque carries details of the fundraising and ends with:
"GENIUS LIKE EGYPT'S MONARCH TIMELY WISE, ERECTS ITS OWN MEMORIAL 'ERE IT DIES."

The northern plaque contains verses from one of Timrod's poems, "Memorial Ode."

The western plaque has a poetic dedication to Timrod's short and tortured life, ending with:
"TO HIS POETIC MISSION HE WAS FAITHFUL TO THE END. IN LIFE AND IN DEATH HE WAS 'NOT DISOBEDIENT UNTO THE HEAVENLY VISION'."
(Again, you've gotta love those double negatives!)

The Carolina granite base is 7 feet tall, the bust is 3 feet. An iron fence surrounds the monument.

The Biography

Henry Timrod (1828-1867) was the son of William Henry, a bookbinder and amateur poet, and Thyrza Prince Timrod. His father died in 1838 from a disease contracted during the Second Seminole War (1835-1843) while serving as captain with the German Fusiliers in Florida. Timrod was educated in the schools of Charleston where he first met his lifelong friend and fellow future poet Paul Hamilton

Hayne (1830-1886). At age 18 he entered Franklin College, which later became the University of Georgia, where he studied literature and fine arts and also began to write poetry. After two years, due to ill health, he was forced to withdraw and returned to Charleston.

Timrod began reading for the law with Charleston attorney James Louis Petigru, but proved unsuited. He then taught school and tutored. His verse began to be published in the "Southern Literary Messenger" and other periodicals. Whenever he had breaks from his teaching or tutoring, he hobnobbed with the city's literary elite who clustered around William Gilmore Simms. He made contributions to the short-lived "Russell's Magazine," edited by his friend Hayne in Charleston.

By the time he was 30, Timrod had been diagnosed with consumption (tuberculosis).

In 1859 Ticknor and Fields of Boston published a small volume of Timrod's poetry simply titled "Poems." Although well reviewed the growing national crisis soon began to dominate the minds of most Americans, including the poet himself.

Timrod's literary output quickly focused on the people and events of the War for Southern Nationality, first as a naïve supporter of the Confederacy and later as a more introspective although still patriotic commentator. This body of work earned him the epithet, "Laureate of the Confederate South."

During the first year of the war, Timrod's fragile health kept him at home, but by early 1862 he enlisted in the 20th South Carolina Regiment to serve as a regimental clerk. Despite his patriotic intentions, his poor health kept him from active duty. After the Battle of Shiloh, he briefly worked as a war correspondent for the Charleston Mercury chronicling the actions of the Confederate Army of the West. By December 1862, ill health forced him to leave his job.

Returning to Charleston, he continued his prolific output of poetry. By August 1863 he was an editor of the Mercury.

In January 1864 Timrod moved to Columbia as part owner and associate editor of the Daily South Carolinian. With a steady job and a little money in the bank he married Kate Goodwin, the longtime object of his affections and his brother-in-law's sister. By the end of the year their son Willie was born. In January 1865 Timrod had a chance encounter with Captain William A. Courtenay. Both were Charlestonians, and Courtenay was an admirer of his work. Timrod expressed disappointment that so little of his work had been published, so Courtenay vowed to help him.

A year and a day after Timrod's wedding, Gen. William T. Sherman's forces attacked Columbia and a devastating fire swept through the city. Ill and financially destitute, Timrod took on the additional burden of caring for his mother, his widowed sister and her four children.

In early October 1865, two of Timrod's sisters died. Later that month son Willie died. Timrod described his son as his "single rosebud in a crown of thorns." His grief further affected his health but he continued to attempt to provide for his family through occasional newspaper work and teaching.

His meager personal possessions were sold. At times Timrod worked as a clerk and occasionally received payment for his poetry.

Timrod was asked to make a poetic contribution to the upcoming memorial observance to honor the Confederate dead at Magnolia Cemetery. He wrote "Memorial Ode," which was sung at the service on June 16, 1866, the fourth anniversary of the Battle of Secessionville. Many consider "Ode" to be his finest work.

In April 1867 Timrod visited his old friend Hayne for several weeks of relaxation and camaraderie. He died October 7, 1867 in Columbia.

The History

Timrod's friend Paul Hayne compiled, edited and in 1873 published "The Poems of Henry Timrod."

In 1898 William A. Courtenay made good on his 30-year-old promise. He organized the Timrod Memorial Association in order to publish a new edition of Timrod's poems as a fundraiser to erect a Charleston memorial. The association contracted with Houghton, Mifflin and Co. to print the Memorial Edition. The book was issued May 1, 1899 at the price of $1.50. Four thousand copies sold during the first 15 months following publication. Additional contributions poured in until the goal of $2,250 was achieved.

The Dedication

On May 1, 1901, the Timrod Art Memorial was dedicated. Two thousand attended the ceremonies. The city's German fraternal and military organizations showed up in force due to Timrod's Teutonic heritage and his father's military service. The ladies of the Memminger School Alumnae Association and the Confederate Home College prepared hundreds of floral arrangements that surrounded and partially covered the base.

Courtenay presided over the ceremonies, made a brief speech and introduced each of the other speakers. Bishop Ellison Capers (See Ellison Capers Tablet — Washington Square) offered the opening prayer, and Mayor J. Adger **S**myth unveiled the monument, covered by an American flag. Smyth congratulated the association and accepted the memorial on behalf of the city.

Henry Austin of New York read "The Memorial Poem," an original composition for the occasion. The poem ended with:

The lyricist of her valiant past,
The limner of her radiant land,
Receives his monument at last,
From Carolina's hand.

Professor Thomas della Torre, Greek and Latin chairman at the College of Charleston, delivered an address titled South Carolina's Debt to Henry Timrod. Former Mayor John F. Ficken delivered a tribute to both Timrod's father and grandfather. Dr. C.S. Vedder gave the benediction.

The Trivia

In 1911 the South Carolina General Assembly adopted Timrod's poem "Carolina" as the state song. Anne Custis Burgess (1874-1910) set the poem's words to music. However, aside from that honor, apparently little attention had been paid to his works for almost 100 years. That is until Albuquerque disc jockey Scott Warmuth discovered at least 10 uncredited lines and phrases from Timrod's poetry in singer Bob Dylan's "Modern Times" album. As they say, "Plagiarism is the sincerest form of flattery." In 1984 South Carolina adopted a second state song, *South Carolina on My Mind,* the work of Henry G. Martin and Buzz Arledge III.

2. Francis Salvador Plaque

The plaque's location hints at the unfortunate obscurity of its dedicatee, Francis Salvador.

The Details

On the park's eastern wall and partially hidden by azaleas is a granite slab with a bronze plaque. Below the scrollwork is the Great Seal of Great Britain. A sovereign is shown conferring liberty on a subject; the word *Nostrae* (of Our Country) is below. *Sigillum Magn Australis Provinciae Nostrae Carolinae* — Great Seal of Our Southern Province of Carolina — encircles the medallion. Below the seal are Salvador's name, his birth and death years and the following assertions:

FIRST JEW IN SOUTH CAROLINA TO
HOLD PUBLIC OFFICE AND TO DIE
FOR AMERICAN INDEPENDENCE

The body of the text recounts the highlights of his brief life in South Carolina. Then follows:

BORN AN ARISTOCRAT, HE BECAME A DEMOCRAT;
AN ENGLISHMAN, HE CAST HIS LOT WITH AMERICA;
TRUE TO HIS ANCIENT FAITH, HE GAVE HIS LIFE FOR
NEW HOPES OF HUMAN LIBERTY AND
UNDERSTANDING.

The plaque is 26 inches x 20 inches at its greatest height and width. The United States Bronze Sign Company of New Hyde Park, N.Y., cast the plaque. The granite slab that holds the plaque has a roughly rounded top. At its greatest height, it is 4 feet, 10 inches.

The Biography

Francis Salvador (1747-1776) was born and educated in England and a member of a wealthy Jewish merchant family. The family's roots were in Portugal, where generations earlier during the Inquisition they probably converted to Christianity to escape persecution. They also adopted the Christian name Salvador, although in all likelihood still practiced their own religion secretly. They relocated to the British Isles.

Salvador married his cousin Sarah, the daughter of his uncle Joseph, a former director of the East India Company and president of the Portuguese congregation in London. Although the reasons are unclear, the family fell on hard times during the 1760s. Joseph was down to his last major asset — 100,000 undeveloped acres on the South Carolina frontier in the Ninety-Six District (modern Greenwood County), which he had purchased in 1755 for £2,000 sterling. When the agent employed to sell or rent the land proved ineffective, Joseph prevailed upon his nephew to take up the task.

In late 1773 Salvador left his wife and four young children behind and made the long, hazardous journey across the Atlantic. (The December 6, 1773, edition of the South Carolina Gazette listed him among the 100 arrivals in Charlestown in the preceding week.) He moved to the backcountry where he hoped his family might recoup its fortune through a combination of land sales and indigo cultivation. He soon established a 7,000-acre plantation, named Corn Acre.

Although the frontier must have been a rather alien environment for this well-educated London gentleman, through some combination of knowledge, common sense and charisma, Salvador became recognized as a natural leader. By late 1774 as South Carolina moved towards self-government by forming the Provincial Congress, the frontier districts were instructed to send representatives to Charlestown.

In the December 26, 1774, edition of the South Carolina Gazette, Salvador was listed among the 10 representatives from the Ninety-Six District. Based on the frequency of his participation in the debates

District. Based on the frequency of his participation in the debates of the First and Second Provincial Congresses, his constituency was well served. In March 1776 South Carolina adopted an independent constitution and the Provincial Congress became the South Carolina General Assembly. Seated in that body, Francis Salvador became the state's and, likely, the nation's first Jewish legislator.

When the Assembly adjourned, Salvador returned to his plantation. For several months he worked tirelessly trying to keep peace on the frontier. But in July Cherokees and their Tory allies attacked frontier settlements. Salvador was called upon to make a 28-mile ride to alert the countryside and gather the militia.

Salvador supported Major Andrew Williamson, commander of the Ninety-Six Militia, in raids against the Cherokees. Learning of a special gathering of tribal leaders, Williamson prepared an early morning surprise attack. Somehow the Cherokees became aware of the impending attack and sprang their own ambush. In an August 1, 1776, engagement, Salvador's regiment was attacked and he was killed. He was 29 years old.

The Dedication

The Salvador Plaque was unveiled November 20, 1950. Its dedication was just one of a series of events celebrating Charleston's Jewish Bicentennial. Several hundred attended the ceremonies. Homer Pace and Hyman Rephan planned the event. The unveiling was presided over by Mrs. Ashley (Eleanor Rose Loeb) Halsey Sr., chairman of the Bicentennial Salvador Plaque Committee. Rabbi Allan Tarshish of Kahal Kadosh Beth Elohim asked the invocation and Rabbi Joseph Rothstein of Brith Sholom Beth Israel pronounced the benediction.

General Charles Summerall, president of the Citadel and principal dedication speaker, eulogized Salvador: "The Jews of Charleston honor themselves when they pay tribute to Salvador. He was almost meteoric in his life and deeds." Paige Halsey and Judith Tobias, descendants of Jewish patriot Lieutenant Abraham Alexander, unveiled the plaque. During the unveiling the 100-man Citadel Cadet Band played "Yankee Doodle." The band, conducted by Leon Freda, played other patriotic songs during the ceremonies.

Trivia

Charleston's Jewish Bicentennial highlighted the little-known fact that the city had the largest urban Jewish population in colonial America. Surprisingly, as late as 1820, it was Charleston, with a population of over 600, not New York City that had the largest number of Jewish residents.

3. Beauregard Memorial Arch

The sheer massiveness of the timeworn memorial reflects the single-mindedness and strength of General Beauregard.

The Details

In the 1904 Charleston Yearbook the caption beneath a photograph of the memorial has a dedication and/or completion date of March 1904. The Beauregard Memorial Committee of the Camp Sumter Chapter, United Confederate Veterans was responsible for the construction of the 12-foot-3-inch-tall Beauregard Memorial Arch.

Four steps are on the front. The lower front sides are composed of alternating blocks of "rock finish" and "all finished" granite. The top of the arch is composed of a diamond pattern of the two different types of granite. Below that the lower portion of the arch holds the following weathered text:

BEAUREGARD
P.G.T. BEAUREGARD
GENERAL
COMMANDING CONFEDERATE FORCES
CHARLESTON, SOUTH CAROLINA
HELD THIS CITY AND HARBOUR
INVIOLATE AGAINST COMBINED ATTACKS
BY LAND AND WATER 1863, 1864, 1865.
THIS MONUMENT IS ERECTED IN HIS HONOUR
BY A GRATEFUL PEOPLE. A.D. 1904

"BEAUREGARD" is in large raised and at one time polished lettering. The remainder of the text is inscribed. It is unclear why "harbor" and "honor" are spelled in the British fashion.

The monument had been visibly leaning for at least 25 years, although was apparently in no danger of toppling. In December 2004, Ram Jack of South Carolina, headquartered in Columbia, righted the leaning monument at no charge to the city. Three corkscrew-like shafts were drilled until something solid was hit, then braces were attached and finally the monument was slowly jacked to an upright position. Part of the bracing can be seen behind the monument.

The Biography

Pierre Gustave Toutant Beauregard (1818-1893) was born at Contreras, his family's plantation in St. Bernard Parish, La. His parents were Jacques Toutant and Helene Judith de Reggio Beauregard. At the age of 8 he was sent to a private school in New Orleans. Later he attended the French School in New York City.

In 1834 Beauregard entered West Point (U.S. Military Academy) and he graduated four years later ranked second in his class. He became a career military officer and engineer. In 1841 Beauregard married Marie Laure Villere. The couple had three children.

Beauregard fought in many of the key battles of the Mexican War, serving on General Winfield Scott's staff.

After the war, Beauregard returned to New Orleans and assumed responsibility for Gulf Coast fortifications. In 1850 his first wife died. A decade later, he married Caroline Deslonde. The couple had no children before her death in 1864.

On January 23, 1861, Beauregard was appointed superintendent of West Point, but served only five days from January 23-28. He was ordered to vacate the post after his Louisiana seceded January 26. He resigned from the U.S. Army and was soon commissioned as a brigadier general in the Confederate Army.

By March 1861 Beauregard was placed in command of Confederate forces in Charleston. And it was in Charleston that a growing political crisis was drawing close to a military solution. The U.S. Army had a small force stationed at Fort Sumter, the keystone to controlling the city's harbor. The situation had taken on some personal undertones for Beauregard because the commander of the Federal forces was his former artillery instructor at West Point, Major Robert Anderson. But despite any personal reservations, when the command was given, student bested mentor in the artillery battle that started in the early morning of April 12, 1861.

With the fort's formal surrender on April 14, Beauregard became the "Hero of Sumter" throughout the Confederate States of America.

Transferred out of Charleston, Beauregard's status as hero seemed to be reaffirmed at the First Battle of Manassas (First Bull Run), where his forces won an impressive victory. He was made a full general at that time. During the Battle of Shiloh (April 6-7, 1862), he was second in command, but assumed command with the death of General Albert Sidney Johnston. Soon after the battle, he left the Army due to illness.

By August 1862, having recovered his health, Beauregard was once again assigned to Charleston. Although he greeted the assignment with some disappointment, the city welcomed the Creole general along with his considerable engineering and artillery skills.

Throughout 1863 Beauregard commanded the Confederate troops that checked the concerted efforts by Union forces to take the city. Under his command great technological experiments in the art of warfare were conducted, including the semi-submersible *David* and the Confederate submarine *H.L. Hunley*, sometimes called the "fish boat," or more ominously, "the peripatetic coffin."

Beauregard was commander when, starting in August 1863, frustrated Union General Quincy Gillmore bombarded the city's civilian population. Beginning in November the city was shelled with varying degrees of intensity for 545 consecutive days, damaging or destroying many buildings.

In April 1864 Beauregard became commander of the Department of North Carolina and Cape Fear. In May he defeated Major

General Benjamin Butler's Army of the James at Bermuda Hundred, Va. A month later his forces held back a Union attack at Petersburg, Va. By November 1864 he was named commander of the Military Division of the West. In February 1865 he assumed command of forces in South Carolina. In April 1865 he was in North Carolina with General Joseph E. Johnston at war's end.

After the Southern Rebellion, Beauregard became president of the New Orleans, Jackson and Mississippi Railroad. He served as manager of the Louisiana State Lottery. He was appointed commissioner of public works in New Orleans and adjutant general of Louisiana.

Beauregard had a deep affection for Charleston. The proof of his attachment became evident shortly after his death. Mayor J.F. Ficken was notified of the following provision in Beauregard's will: "I give the City of Charleston, S.C., if acceptable to it, the sword which was presented to me by some ladies of New Orleans in 1861 for the capture of Fort Sumter." A distinguished delegation of five, headed by former mayors William A. Courtenay and W. Porcher Miles, was dispatched to New Orleans to accept the sword from Beauregard's family. It remains one of the city's most cherished possessions and on display, along with a fine portrait of Beauregard by George P.A. Healy, in the nearby City Council Chamber.

4. John Christie Plaque

A tribute to a Masonic founding father reminds us that not every American fought for independence. Many remained loyal to their king, and some paid with their lives.

The Details and Dedication

The 36-inch-by-28-inch bronze plaque honors Michigan Masonic Lodge founder John Christie. It is attached to a 4-foot-7-inch tapered granite slab. It was unveiled April 24, 1961 by a number of Masonic officials including W. Wallace Kent, grand master of Masons in Michigan.

The Biographical Sketch

Much of the life of John Christie is a mystery. In 1758 he joined the 60th Royal American Foot Regiment. During Pontiac's Rebellion (1763-1766) Ensign Christie was in command of fewer than three-dozen soldiers at Fort Presque Isle, near modern day Erie, Pa. By June 15, 1763, the fort was under siege by a force of Senecas, Ottawas, Wyandots and Chippewas. On June 20, 1763, the fort was set afire and the troops were forced to evacuate. Only Christie and two others escaped alive.

In September 1772 Christie became a lieutenant in the Second Battalion. During the American Revolution he was in the 4th Battalion, becoming a captain in September 1775 when the 4th Battalion was re-raised (both the 3rd and 4th had been disbanded in 1763). He fought gallantly against Spanish troops at the Battle of Fort Charlotte during the British defense of Mobile in 1780.

According to the plaque, Christie died June 1782 in Antigua, West Indies. Although it's unclear why, his remains were returned to Charlestown and a funeral was conducted August 10, 1782, at St. Philip's Church. Records indicate a burial at Hempstead Hill, modern Hampstead Mall, although no gravesite can be located.

However, as far as the plaque is concerned, Christie's claim to fame derives directly from being the founder and first worshipful master of the earliest documented Masonic Lodge west of the Alleghenies. George Harlson, grand master of the Provincial Grand Lodge of New York, authorized the founding of a lodge in Detroit on April 27, 1764.

PRAYER COMPOSED BY ELLISON CAPERS
EPISCOPAL BISHOP — CONFEDERATE SOLDIER

"ALMIGHTY GOD, OUR HEAVENLY FATHER, WE ADORE THY LOVE AND PROVIDENCE IN THE HISTORY OF OUR COUNTRY, AND ESPECIALLY WOULD WE THANK THEE FOR OUR CONFEDERATE HISTORY.

"WE THANK THEE FOR ITS PURE RECORD OF VIRTUE, VALOR AND FOR THE INSPIRING REFLECTION THAT DESPITE ITS BITTER DISAPPOINTMENTS AND SORROWS IT PROCLAIMS FOR US TO ALL THE WORLD THAT WE CAME THROUGH ITS YEARS OF TRIAL AND STRUGGLES WITH OUR BATTERED SHIELDS PURE, OUR CHARACTER AS A PATRIOTIC AND COURAGEOUS PEOPLE UNTARNISHED AND NOTHING TO REGRET IN OUR DEFENSE OF THE RIGHTS AND HONOR OF OUR SOUTHLAND.

"GIVE US GRACE, OUR HEAVENLY FATHER, FAITHFULLY TO ACCEPT THY WILL CONCERNING US, AND MAKE US ALL TO GLORIFY THEE IN A SINCERE OBEDIENCE TO THY HOLY COMMANDMENTS, THROUGH THE MERITS, MEDIATION OF THY SON, OUR ONLY SAVIOR, JESUS CHRIST."

ERECTED BY THE SOUTH CAROLINA DIVISION
UNITED DAUGHTERS OF THE CONFEDERACY

5. Ellison Capers Tablet

A prayer is an appropriate way to remember Ellison Capers, military leader in time of war, religious leader in a time of peace, a lifelong man of faith.

The Dedication and Details

The 28-inch-by-36-inch bronze tablet designed by the Ashley Crest Cemetery Corporation of Charleston is attached directly to the eastern wall. It holds a prayer written by Bishop Ellison Capers, a former Confederate general. It is the official prayer of the South Carolina Division of the United Daughters of the Confederacy.

On October 11, 1968, the division presented the plaque to the city at a dedication ceremony. The Bishop's great-grandson Navy Commander Ellison Capers unveiled it during the division's annual convention.

The Biography

Ellison Capers (1837-1908) was the son of William, a Methodist bishop, and Susan McGill Capers. He was raised and educated in Charleston. He graduated from the Citadel in 1857 and remained at the school an additional year as a mathematics instructor. After serving one year as principal at Mount Zion College in Winnsboro,

S.C. he returned to The Citadel as an assistant professor of mathematics. He married Charlotte "Lottie" Palmer in 1859. They had nine children.

With the outbreak of Mr. Lincoln's War imminent, Capers was elected major of a volunteer regiment that later took part in the bombardment of Fort Sumter on April 12 and 13, 1861. By November 1861 he resigned his position at the Citadel and, along with Colonel C.H. Stevens, formed the 24th South Carolina Infantry Regiment, serving as lieutenant colonel.

In a June 3, 1862, skirmish on James Island, while leading the 24th South Carolina and other troops, Capers and his men captured men of three Union regiments. Two weeks later at the Battle of Secessionville his regiment held the Confederate left flank and helped to repulse a number of Union attacks.

In May 1863 after two years of fighting in the Carolinas, the regiment, then part of a brigade under the command of Brigadier General S.R. "States Rights" Gist, was ordered west to support the relief of Vicksburg. Although they arrived too late for the Battle of Raymond (May 12), two days later the South Carolinians saw action at the Battle of Jackson against Union troops commanded by General Ulysses S. Grant. Although the battle was a Union victory, the companies under Capers' command won high praise. He sustained a wound from which he quickly recovered.

On September 20, 1863, Gist's command fought at Chickamauga, where Capers was again wounded. He recovered sufficiently to lead his regiment two months later at Missionary Ridge. In January 1864, he was promoted to colonel and commanded his regiment throughout the Atlanta campaign. The high point of his participation came September 1, 1864 at Jonesboro when his outfit held the extreme right of Lieutenant General William J. Hardee's corps throughout an afternoon series of attacks. At the Battle of Franklin, November 30, 1864, he was again wounded and General Gist was killed. On March 1, 1865, having recovered from his latest wound, he was promoted to brigadier general, becoming one of four Citadel graduates to achieve that rank during the course of the war. He was then assigned permanent command of Gist's brigade.

During the course of "this strange struggle," as he termed the War of the North and South, Capers maintained and strengthened his Christian faith. Although he was convinced to run for public office immediately after the war (and won the office of secretary of state in 1866), within a year he entered the ministry of the Episcopal Church and served Christ Church, Greenville. In 1887 he was called to Trinity Church, Columbia. In 1889 he received his D.D. from the University of South Carolina. On July 20, 1893, he was elected the seventh Bishop of the South Carolina Diocese of the Protestant Episcopal Church. In 1904 he was elected chancellor of the University of the South at Sewanee, Tenn.

Until his death Capers served as chaplain general for the United Confederate Veterans. In this capacity he gave orations and prayers at the dedication ceremonies of many Confederate memorials. Although his principal role was to honor the Confederate dead, he also looked upon those occasions as opportunities to promote harmony and reconciliation.

The Trivia

The Capers family has three generations of bishops. William Capers, Ellison's father, was a Methodist bishop. Both Ellison and his son William T. Capers were Episcopal bishops.

6. Governor Robert Gibbes Plaque

Robert Gibbes' brief resumé offers little insight about this controversial early governor.

The Details

The 36-inch-by-28-inch plaque recounts the highlights of Proprietary Governor Robert Gibbes' governmental/political career in South Carolina. The plaque is attached directly to the wall that forms the park's eastern boundary. The insignia of the S.C. Society of Colonial Dames XVII Century is featured in bas-relief. Newman Brothers Inc. of Cincinnati, Ohio fabricated the plaque.

The Biography

Robert Gibbes (1644-1715) was born in Sandwich, Kent, England, the son of Robert and Mary Coventry Gibbes. While still a young man he and other family members moved to Barbados. In 1665 he was among the "Barbadian Adventurers" who reached an agreement with the Lords Proprietors to establish a colony in the Carolinas. Both he and his brother Thomas served in the governing assembly of the short-lived Cape Fear settlement.

By 1672 following the settlement of Charles Towne, Gibbes began to accumulate vast landholdings in South Carolina. From the beginning there were strong familial, commercial and political connections between South Carolina and Barbados. For a time, like many Barbadians, Gibbes moved back and forth between the two colonies before finally settling in Charles Towne.

In 1684 Gibbes was appointed the colony's sheriff. He represented Colleton County in the lower house of assembly (1692-1694). In 1698 he was appointed the Colleton family's deputy in the colony, making him a member of the Grand Council. Ten years later, although there is no evidence he had legal training, he was named chief justice.

In 1710 Gibbes was again serving as proprietary deputy when Governor Edward Tynte died. Tynte's instructions were that the three proprietary deputies in the colony at the time (Gibbes; Thomas Broughton, former governor Nathaniel Johnson's son-in-law; and Fortescue Turberville) choose an interim governor from among their number. The initial vote awarded the position to Broughton, but later the same day Turberville changed his vote, making Gibbes governor. Within weeks Turberville died but not before revealing that Gibbes had bribed him.

Gibbes became a lame duck as the colony awaited the Lords Proprietors' decision on his malfeasance. In 1711 when Tuscarora Indians attacked New Bern, N.C., he twice dispatched expeditions comprised of South Carolina militiamen and Indian allies to suppress them. In March 1712 the Proprietors replaced him with Charles Craven.

The Dedication

The Governor Robert Gibbes Chapter, South Carolina Society of Colonial Dames 17th Century, dedicated the plaque on June 26, 1999. A number of Gibbes' descendants, members of the Gibbes Chapter and other chapter members were on hand for the ceremony. Mrs. Winfred D. (Esther) Cope, state chaplain, provided the invocation and the benediction.

Mrs. Lawrence A. (Elizabeth) Bryant, flag custodian, led both the Pledge of Allegiance and the American's Creed. Mrs. Penrod G. (Betta) Hepfer, president of the Gibbes Chapter, welcomed those assembled for the event. Mrs. Joseph W. (Mary Frances) Coker, state president, responded to the greetings received prior to the ceremony. Mrs. Willie (Sabra) Moseley, state first vice president, introduced the honored guests. Mrs. Frank P. (Mincy) Copeland Jr. provided a historical background of Governor Gibbes. Mrs. Leonard (Annette) Metz, first vice president of the Gibbes Chapter, dedicated the marker. Mrs. Coker and Jack McGuire unveiled the marker in memory of Mrs. Margaret Gibbes Schiro. Robert Rosen, chairman of the Arts and History Commission, accepted the marker on behalf of the city.

In her will Margaret Gibbes Schiro, one of Gibbes' descendants, left $1,300 to the chapter for the marker. Jack McGuire represented the late Mrs. Schiro at the ceremony. Following the dedication a reception was held at Huguenot Heritage Hall.

7. Elizabeth Jackson Monument

A plain granite monument understates one woman's contributions to the fight for independence.

The Details and Dedication

On April 30, 1954, the Rebecca Motte Chapter, South Carolina Daughters of the American Revolution, dedicated the 3-foot-10-inch monument as a memorial to Elizabeth Jackson, American patriot and

IN MEMORY OF
ELIZABETH HUTCHINSON
JACKSON
MOTHER OF
ANDREW JACKSON
PRESIDENT OF THE U.S. 1829 – 1837
WHO GAVE HER LIFE IN THE
CAUSE OF INDEPENDENCE
WHILE NURSING REVOLUTIONARY
SOLDIERS IN CHARLES TOWN
AND IS BURIED IN CHARLESTON
ERECTED BY
REBECCA MOTTE CHAPTER D.A.R.

mother of Andrew Jackson. The inscription connects her with her famous son and gives details of her sacrifices and death.

The Rev. Edwin B. Clipp read the invocation and benediction. Dr. Bernard L. Poole, associate professor of history and government at the College of Charleston, made the dedicatory speech. Additional speakers were Mrs. James T. Owen, SCDAR regent, Mrs. Herbert A. Smith, regent of the Rebecca Motte Chapter, and Mrs. J.V. Nielsen Jr., chapter historian. Margaret Smith and Caroline Speissegger performed the unveiling. Mayor William McG. Morrison accepted the monument on behalf of the city.

The Biographies

Elizabeth Hutchinson Jackson (circa 1740-1781) was the mother of the nation's seventh president, Andrew Jackson (1767-1845). In 1765 she, her husband and their young sons Hugh and Robert left

County Antrim, Ireland. After landing in either Charlestown or one of the ports along the Delaware River, the family made its way to the Waxhaws, a frontier settlement along the boundary between the Carolinas. They joined many other Scots-Irish settlers in the area.

Andrew Sr. died in 1767 around the time his third son and namesake was born. Although it is unclear on which side of the border Jackson was born and despite the fact that both North and South Carolina claim him, Andrew Jackson described himself as a South Carolinian. Elizabeth became the housekeeper for her semi-invalid sister, Jane, and her brother-in-law, James Crawford.

When the Revolution came to the Waxhaws, the eldest son, Hugh, rode with patriot leader Colonel William Richardson Davie. Hugh died of heat exhaustion at the Battle of Stono Ferry in June 1779.

In May 1780 war came even closer to home when Banastre Tarleton's British Legion mauled a detachment of Continental troops commanded by Colonel Abraham Buford. In what came to be known as "Buford's Massacre," many American soldiers, either attempting to surrender or lying wounded on the ground, were slaughtered. Many of the survivors were brought to the nearby Waxhaws Presbyterian Church. Among those who cared for them were Elizabeth, Robert and Andrew Jackson. Subsequently, the family was forced into hiding whenever Tory or British units passed through the settlement.

Around this time, 13-year-old Andrew and his 15-year-old brother, Robert, joined Davie's unit. Although non-combatants, the boys were close to the fighting when, in early August 1780, Colonel Davie and General Thomas Sumter engaged and defeated the enemy at Hanging Rock. This triumph was soon forgotten with Cornwallis' resounding victory at the Battle of Camden later in the month. With their settlement in the path of the victorious British forces, the Jacksons fled to safety in Charlotte, N.C., where they stayed for the next four months.

Back home in April 1781 the settlement was surprised by a party of British light dragoons and mounted infantry. The Jackson brothers were among those taken captive. This led to a confrontation with a British officer. When Andrew was told to clean an officer's boots, the lad refused, demanding to be treated as a prisoner of war. In response the officer slashed at him with a sword. Andrew threw up his left hand, saving his life but acquiring deep gashes in his hand and forehead. Robert's refusal to follow the officer's order led to a severe blow to the head.

The brothers were marched to Camden where they were separated and penned with other prisoners. Smallpox broke out in the camp and both brothers contracted the deadly disease. Soon after the Battle of Hobrick's Hill, Elizabeth and others arranged for a prisoner exchange that included her sons. She took them home but days later, 16-year-old Robert died.

Throughout the summer Elizabeth nursed her remaining son back to health. During Andrew's convalescence, his mother became aware of the plight of the Crawfords, her nephews and other prisoners of war being held on prison ships in Charlestown harbor. Leaving Andrew in the care of kin, she accompanied other Waxhaw women on a journey to the British-occupied city. They brought food, medicine, clothing and nursing skills to their desperate countrymen. In November, not long after her arrival in the city, Elizabeth became another casualty of war, succumbing to cholera.

In many ways, Elizabeth Jackson's life, filled with tragedy and sacrifice, symbolized the largely anonymous role played by women during the Revolution. It was only the fame of her youngest son that brought her story to the forefront.

The Trivia

The first presidential assassination occurred April 14, 1865, when John Wilkes Booth shot Abraham Lincoln during a performance at Ford's Theatre. Lincoln died the following day. However, the first assassination attempt occurred January 30, 1835, when Richard Lawrence (circa 1800-1861), a mentally unstable house painter, fired two pistols at Jackson. Amazingly, both misfired and Jackson, who had previously been wounded in duels, was uninjured. The attempt was made in the rotunda of the Capitol where Jackson was attending the funeral for Representative Warren Ransom Davis of South Carolina.

On April 11, 1835, Lawrence's trial began in U.S. Circuit Court in Washington, D.C. The prosecuting attorney was Francis Scott Key, of *Star Spangled Banner* fame. The jury took only five minutes to find Lawrence not guilty by reason of insanity. The remainder of his life was spent confined in a variety of hospitals and mental institutions.

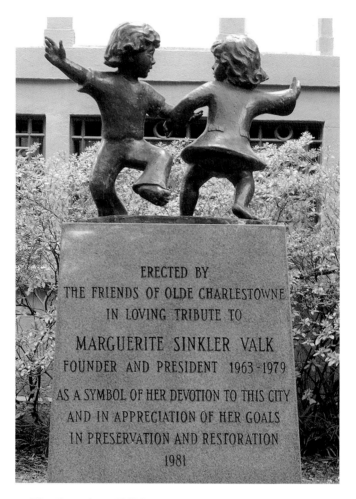

ERECTED BY
THE FRIENDS OF OLDE CHARLESTOWNE
IN LOVING TRIBUTE TO

MARGUERITE SINKLER VALK
FOUNDER AND PRESIDENT 1963-1979

AS A SYMBOL OF HER DEVOTION TO THIS CITY
AND IN APPRECIATION OF HER GOALS
IN PRESERVATION AND RESTORATION
1981

8. The Dancing Children

Two carefree, young children are dancing merrily. This lovely piece of artwork symbolizes the twin passions of a Charleston woman's life: To beautify the homes of her customers and preserve the eroding beauty of Charleston's historic buildings.

The Details and a Brief History

The whimsical sculpture is a memorial to interior designer and preservationist Marguerite Sinkler Valk. At their greatest height, the bronze children are 21 inches. The 3-foot-3-inch pedestal includes a 6-inch base. The Friends of Olde Charlestowne dedicated the sculpture in 1981:

AS A SYMBOL OF HER DEVOTION TO THIS CITY AND IN APPRECIATION OF HER GOALS IN PRESERVATION AND RESTORATION.

Following Valk's death her friends, family and Friends of Olde Charlestowne, an organization she founded, wanted to honor her many civic contributions. One of Willard Hirsch's sculptures was chosen as an appropriate memorial. Note his signature and the year "1976" under the little girl. The bronze was originally proposed as a drinking fountain reminiscent of Hirsch's the "Little Dancer" in White Point Garden. However, since there was already one in the park, the plan was altered.

At the September 23, 1980, City Council meeting, a report was submitted by members of the Arts and History Commission indicating their recommendation to accept "Little Bronze" as a gift. The commission additionally reported that the city would entail no expense by accepting the sculpture. Council adopted the report.

The Biography

Marguerite Sinkler Valk (1894-1979) was one of four children born to Daniel LaSaine and Ellen Simons Hall Sinkler. In 1917 she married Courtney Valk, stepson of former mayor William A. Courtney. The couple had one child, also named Marguerite.

Valk was Charleston born and bred but starting in the 1930s she began to be recognized as one of the nation's leading interior decorators. In a March 17, 1949, article in the News and Courier, she described her career as simply, "Doing what comes naturally." Until the late 1920s she said she had never worked, never thought about working and had no particular training. Initially she opened an antique shop and later to satisfy the needs of her customers she applied her considerable talents to the field of interior design. She was self-taught, extensively studying styles of the 18th and 19th centuries.

Soon Valk's flair and creativity were recognized beyond the Charleston area. Her clientele included the wealthy of Newport, Boston, New York, and Jekyll Island. Among her many clients was Washington newspaper publisher Evalyn Walsh McLean, one-time owner of the Hope Diamond. Perhaps Valk's biggest project was redecorating 400 rooms in four months as assistant decorator for the St. Regis Hotel in New York City.

At various times, Valk owned design shops at 85 Church Street in Charleston, on Whiskey Road in Aiken, S.C., and in Newport, R.I. A highlight of her career came in 1942 when she received an American Institute of Design award for her work on a Vanderbilt mansion in Newport.

Regardless of where Valk was working, her heart was always in Charleston. In her later years, she devoted much of her time and energy to the Preservation Society of Charleston, the Garden Club of Charleston, the Charleston County League of Women Voters, the Historic Charleston Foundation, the Gibbes Museum of Art and the Charleston Museum. She was a founder and only president of Friends of Olde Charlestowne (1963-1979), an organization that raised funds for a variety of preservation and restoration projects.

9. Washington Memorial Tree

The brief details on the plaque tell a story that is no longer true.

The Dedication

On February 23, 1932 a white oak sapling from Mount Vernon was planted on the site, as part of the state celebrations commemorating the bicentennial of George Washington's birth. Rain had delayed the ceremony, originally scheduled for the previous day (the actual bicentennial.)

Julius M. Visanka, president of the Charleston Chamber of Commerce, presided at the exercises. The Rev. Harold Thomas, rector of St. Luke's Protestant Episcopal Church, made the invocation. Daniel Ravenel, state chairman of the George Washington Bicentennial Commission, presented the tree to the city and Mayor pro tem J. Albert Von Dohlen accepted the gift. The white oak was obtained through the efforts of Virginia Leigh Porcher of Charleston, a vice regent of the Mount Vernon Association.

In his address Von Dohlen praised South Carolinian Ann Pamela Cunningham, who had devoted much of her life to the preservation of Mount Vernon. Von Dohlen went on to imagine the distant future: "This white oak secured from the Mount Vernon home of Washington in time will grow to full strength just as we as a nation have become powerful among the people of the world, and in its sturdy

strength will our children find symbolized that strength of character which was Washington's." (Ah, yes, a very inspirational sentiment. . .)

Later the Rebecca Motte Chapter, South Carolina Daughters of the American Revolution, commemorated the event by placing a low marker with attached plaque on the site.

Unfortunately, Von Dohlen's prediction never came true. On September 29, 1938, several tornadoes touched down in the city causing 32 deaths, 300 injuries, $2 million in damage and the destruction of all the park's trees. With the aid of U.S. Forest Service equipment, live oaks 10 to 15 years old, and palmettos were transplanted, replacing the elms, Washingtonia palms and the sapling. The impostor behind the marker is, alas, just another live oak.

10. George Washington Statue

An elegantly dressed George Washington stares toward the West and to the future of his country.

The Details

The 8-foot Washington statue stands atop a 7-foot-3-inch yellow brick base previously used for the William Pitt statue. Note "J.N. Michel sculpt 1999" inscribed in the statue's base.

The only clue to the statue's identity can be discovered by backing away in the direction of the park's Meeting Street entrance until WASHINGTON can be seen in the bronze's base. No Washington plaques have graced the pedestal but a brief biography is planned:

GEORGE WASHINGTON WAS BORN IN VIRGINIA ON FEBRUARY 22, 1732. AS A BOY, HE EXCELLED IN FIELD SPORTS, AND THOUGH HIS FORMAL EDUCATION WAS LIMITED, HE EXHIBITED SKILL IN MATHEMATICS AND SURVEYING.

IN THE FRENCH AND INDIAN WAR, THOUGH ONLY 23, COLONEL WASHINGTON DEMONSTRATED UNFLINCHING COURAGE AND EXTRAORDINARY LEADERSHIP UNDER FIRE.

DURING THE REVOLUTIONARY WAR, GENERAL WASHINGTON COMMANDED THE CONTINENTAL ARMY AGAINST SUPERIOR FORCES. HE DEVISED THE STRATEGY OF MARCHING ON THE BRITISH IN VIRGINIA WHILE THE FRENCH FLEET PREVENTED AN

ESCAPE BY SEA. WASHINGTON TRAPPED
GENERAL CORNWALLIS AT YORKTOWN IN 1781,
CAPTURING 7,000 TROOPS AND WINNING
AMERICAN INDEPENDENCE.

AS A VIRGINIA DELEGATE TO THE CONSTITUTIONAL
CONVENTION IN PHILADELPHIA IN 1787,
WASHINGTON PROVIDED THE MORAL AUTHORITY AND QUIET

LEADERSHIP NEEDED TO FACILITATE COMPROMISES. EVEN AT
THIS TIME, HE WAS KNOWN AS A "FOUNDING FATHER."
FOLLOWING RATIFICATION OF THE CONSTITUTION, HE
WAS UNANIMOUSLY ELECTED THE FIRST PRESIDENT AND
INAUGURATED IN NEW YORK ON APRIL 30, 1789.

PRESIDENT WASHINGTON TOURED THE SOUTHERN STATES
IN 1791. HIS ENORMOUS PERSONAL POPULARITY SERVED AS
A SIGNIFICANT FORCE IN BINDING THE FORMER THIRTEEN
COLONIES INTO A SINGLE NATION. ON MAY 2, HE LANDED AT
PRIOLEAU WHARF, ONE BLOCK SOUTH OF THE EXCHANGE
AND CUSTOMS HOUSE. WHILE IN CHARLESTON, PRESIDENT
WASHINGTON MET WITH NUMEROUS POLITICIANS, PLANTERS
AND MERCHANTS, WORSHIPPED AT ST. MICHAEL'S AND ST.
PHILIP'S CHURCHES, SPOKE TO VARIOUS GATHERINGS OF
CITIZENS AND ATTENDED SEVERAL BALLS HELD IN HIS HONOR.

HE ALSO ENJOYED THE HOSPITALITY OF TWO FRATERNAL
GROUPS OF WHICH HE WAS A MEMBER—THE MASONS AND THE
SOCIETY OF THE CINCINNATI. IN HIS DIARY, HE MADE SEVERAL
COMPLIMENTARY NOTES ABOUT CHARLESTONIANS. REFERRING
TO A CONCERT HELD AT THE EXCHANGE, WASHINGTON
REMARKED THAT "THERE WERE AT LEAST 400 LAD[IE]S—THE
NUMBER AND APPEARANCE OF WHICH. EXCEEDED ANY THING
OF THE KIND I HAVE EVER SEEN."

WASHINGTON WAS UNANIMOUSLY REELECTED IN 1792.
CONFRONTED WITH THE COMPETING PHILOSOPHIES
OF THE NORTHERN BUSINESSMEN AND THE SOUTHERN
PLANTERS, PRESIDENT WASHINGTON HAD A UNIQUE ABILITY
TO RECOGNIZE AND PROMOTE THE BEST OF EACH. LEAVING
OFFICE AFTER TWO TERMS, HE ESTABLISHED THE TRADITION
OF PEACEFUL TRANSITION OF POWER. RETIRING TO MOUNT
VERNON, HE MANAGED HIS PLANTATION, ENTERTAINED MANY
VISITORS AND REMAINED A VALUED POLITICAL AND MILITARY
ADVISOR UNTIL HIS DEATH ON DECEMBER 14, 1799.

OF HIS MANY ACHIEVEMENTS, HE IS MOST LOVED FOR
HIS HONESTY. GEORGE WASHINGTON'S REPUTATION FOR

The History

Remarkably, the newest feature in Washington Square, aside from a new drinking fountain installed in late April 2007, is the George Washington statue. The statue commemorates Washington's week-long visit to Charleston in May 1791 during his Southern Tour, an opportunity to visit parts of North and South Carolina and Georgia.

In 1992 Charleston businessman Bill Gilliam shared his idea of honoring the nation's first president with Mayor Joseph P. Riley Jr. Soon afterward Riley tapped General (Ret.) William Westmoreland (1914-2005) to serve as chairman of the Committee to Bring George Washington Back to Charleston.

Felix W. de Weldon (1907-2003) was initially chosen as sculptor. He is best known for the Marine Corps War Memorial (Flag Raising on Iwo Jima). De Weldon suggested recycling the Pitt pedestal, which had been vacant since 1985 when the statue was moved to the Charleston Museum. The Pitt statue is now on display in the lobby of the Charleston County Judicial Center at 100 Broad Street. By December 1993, due to a number of factors, John Michel replaced de Weldon. Somewhere along the line, however, the project foundered. By late 1998, despite continued quarterly meetings, the committee had made little progress.

J. Grahame Long, education coordinator at the Old Exchange, began exploring the idea of some type of commemoration of the bicentennial of Washington's death December 14, 1999, at the instigation of his supervisor, Frances McCarthy. He mentioned the idea to his friend Carol Ezell-Gilson, who, as docent/historian of the Council Chamber and transcription secretary of the Arts and History Commission, was aware of the committee's efforts. She contacted John Michel to determine if he was still available for the project. He was. Ezell-Gilson also advised Mayor Riley of the impending deadline and asked if the city would help finance it. The Mayor promised the city's support. Ezell-Gilson and Long contacted attorney and Committee Vice Chair William C. Cleveland, who quickly made them part of the effort.

Although numerous people were involved, a Committee of Five,

composed of Cleveland, Ezell-Gilson, Long, General Joseph C. Hurteau and Charles W. Waring III, guided the project to a successful conclusion. Cleveland played a key role in making many of the major fund-raising presentations.

Michel spent five months sculpting Washington's image. The bronze casting, the work of the Ward Sculptural Arts Foundry of Atlanta, took an additional three months.

Just prior to the statue's installation, structural engineer Robert Shoolbred of Charleston inspected the brick pedestal at no cost and found it to be sound.

The cost of the project was $165,000. The city contributed $25,000; Charleston County gave $40,000; the South Carolina Legacy Trust Fund's portion was $50,000; and the remainder came from various organizations including the Washington Light Infantry and the Society of the Cincinnati; private donations and project fundraisers. The largest of the fundraisers was May 25, 1999, at Jimmy Dengate's pub, 5 Cumberland Street. The admission price ($5) and free food and drink enticed hundreds to come and buy raffle tickets. The fund-raiser also offered attendees the opportunity to meet General Westmoreland.

The Dedication

On December 14, 1999, a procession marched from the Old Exchange Building — Charleston's original city hall and the center of the celebrations during Washington's 1791 visit — to Washington Square.

As the marchers approached the park, St. Michael's bells pealed and the Charleston Symphony Brass Quintet played *A Fanfare of Horns.*

Several hundred people gathered for the ceremonies. William Cleveland welcomed the attendees with, "It is only fitting that we should gather here today in the country's foremost city to honor our country's foremost hero."

In the invocation, the Very Rev. William McKeachie, dean of the Cathedral Church of St. Luke and St. Paul, asked for the promotion of Washington's "collective wisdom, virtue and morality, indispensable to this form of government."

The Men's Chorus of the Mount Zion AME Church, conducted by Alphonso Brown, sang the *National Anthem.*

Elizabeth Jenkins Young, well-known Charleston preservationist and tour guide, added levity to the ceremonies: "People ask me, 'What was it like, Liz, when George Washington visited Charleston?' The first thing I say is, 'I wasn't there!'"

General Westmoreland gave the crowd an overview of the project. He then presented the *maquette* (model) of the statue to J. Grahame Long, who accepted on behalf of the Old Exchange.

Charleston County Council Chairman Barret Lawrimore also spoke.

In his speech Mayor Riley recognized the instrumental role of sculptor John Michel. Riley also welcomed the nation's first president back to Charleston, reminding those gathered of Washington's legacy contained in Henry "Light Horse Harry" Lee's eulogy: "To the memory of the Man, first in war, first in peace and first in the hearts of his countrymen."

Carol Ezell-Gilson and Charles W. Waring III pulled aside the black drape, unveiling the statue.

The finale included a Marine Corps 21-gun rifle salute followed by the playing of a *Fanfare for George Washington*, an original piece of music by Dr. Edward Hart, professor at the College of Charleston.

Following the ceremonies, attendees viewed a special George Washington exhibit at the nearby South Carolina Historical Society building. The sculptor conducted an informal question-and-answer session in the City Council Chamber. A reception organized by Ezell-Gilson and presented by the Old Exchange recognized the project's major financial contributors.

The Final Detail

You might wonder why there are no plaques mounted on the pedestal yet? Well, folks, a brief recap: Remember, it took from 1881 until 1999 to get a Washington statue erected in Washington Square. So, a little more patience is in order. Right?

The Trivia

The choice of Washington's death as the dedication date may seem odd but there is a precedent. The plaque on the harbor side of the Old Exchange Building at 122 East Bay Street that highlights the building's extensive history, including Washington's visit, was dedicated December 14, 1899, the centennial of his death.

11. Centennial Time Capsule

The inscription immediately sparks your imagination and prompts a question: What's in there?

The Details

Approaching the Washington Light Infantry monument from Broad Street, note the low granite marker. The inscription reads:

FORT SUMTER
CENTENNIAL
APRIL 12, 1961
TIME CAPSULE
TO BE OPENED
APRIL 12, 2061

The capsule is a suitcase-sized, galvanized metal container. It is within a larger metal box and both are covered with a layer of concrete.

Now, this is where I need to divide the reading audience. If you are young enough to attend the reopening ceremony, stop reading at this point. I don't want to ruin the surprise.

However, if either superannuation or death might prevent your attendance, this is a partial listing of the 35 items contained within. A complete script of and tickets to "the Charleston Story," a historical pageant; Mayor Gaillard's proclamation of the Fort Sumter Centennial; newspaper special sections and editions; a tape recording of "Secession Day 1860," a WCSC-TV historical re-creation; a Fort Sumter commemorative plate; a South Carolina Centennial Commission medal composed of recovered metal from Union shells; a commemorative bow tie; a replica Confederate cap; a first-day cover of the Fort Sumter stamp; letters of greeting from the mayor and governor; and a publication of the Carolina Art Association.

The Dedication

The dedication and burial of the capsule on April 19, 1961, brought to a close the week-long observance of the 100th anniversary of the firing on Fort Sumter.

Dignitaries and spectators gathered around the Washington Light Infantry Monument for "The Next Hundred Years Day." J. Kenneth Rentiers arranged the ceremony and Henry Deas, chairman of the Fort Sumter Centennial, was master of ceremonies.

The Rev. Charles Wessinger, pastor of St. Andrew's Lutheran Church, asked the invocation. Mayor J. Palmer Gaillard spoke of the necessity of adapting to changing times, citing the changes Charleston had undergone in the century since the outbreak of the War of Southern Secession. He noted that differences of opinion were part of human nature. And he called upon those present to: ". . . join me in the hopes that these differences will be settled without arms and then when this capsule is opened our country will still be united."

Mrs. J.C. Long, chairman of the Charleston Confederate War Centennial Commission, presented the time capsule to the mayor. The Bishop England High School Band, directed by Michael J. Farmer, played for the occasion.

12. Washington Light Infantry Monument

A spectacular obelisk dominates the park and pays homage to the men of the Washington Light Infantry who fought and died during the War for States Rights.

The Details

The Washington Light Infantry obelisk stands an estimated 32 feet tall on an octagonal knoll that is edged with stone. The perimeter is planted in seasonal flowers and the remainder in grass. A bluestone walkway approaches the obelisk from the south side. Three square granite bases of decreasing size provide both steps and a platform for the monument. The four sides of the three bases are inscribed with the names of a mere 12 of the 43 battles in which members of the unit fought during the War Between the States. The three bases and the monument's three granite sections represent the three different companies in which Washington Light Infantry's members served.

The monument's four faces are graced with five bronze plaques. The southern face holds two plaques. The higher one features a bas-relief of the state seal. (For a detailed interpretation of the state seal's symbolism, see The Defenders of Fort Moultrie—White Point Garden.)

Note the name of the founder — The Henry-Bonnard Bronze Co. New York 1891 — beautifully etched in the lower left hand corner of the plaque. The lower plaque has a bas-relief of the Washington Light Infantry's coat of arms, verses from "Christmas Hymn" by Dr. John Dickson Bruns and the monument's dedication. The inscription ends with *Fortuna non mutat genus*, which means, "Circumstance does not change our origin." Fifty percent of the metal in these two plaques was salvaged from Marion Artillery fieldpieces.

The south-facing plaques were the only ones completed for the dedication. The others were added in 1894.

The eastern plaque offers verses from "the Conquered Banner," by Rev. Abram J. Ryan and designates the roll of the 36 men who died during service in Company B, 25th Regiment, South Carolina Volunteers. A bas-relief of crossed Confederate flags is at the top of the eastern, western and northern plaques.

The northern plaque contains verses from the "Broken Battalions," by Paul Hayne, and the roll of the 39 men who died serving in Company A, Hampton Legion, Infantry.

The western plaque offers verses from "the Unknown Dead," by Henry Timrod, and lists the 39 dead from Company A, 25th Regiment, South Carolina Volunteers.

The History

The Washington Light Infantry was named for the first U.S. president and organized in July 1807 after the "Chesapeake-Leopard Incident," when the British warship *Leopard* attacked the American vessel *Chesapeake*. Some members of the American crew were impressed by the British. The regiment first mustered during the War of 1812 and served in all major American military conflicts through World War II. Today the Washington Light Infantry is one of 83 associations in the Centennial Legion of Historic Military Commands pledged to keep alive their traditions and preserve their military records.

The monument is dedicated to all 414 men who served and, in particular, the 114 "unreturning brave" who died during the Cruel War. The monument replaced an earlier one that the Washington Light Infantry had erected at Magnolia Cemetery in 1870. In 1890 the city contributed the site and the Washington Light Infantry raised $13,000 to finance the project.

The Dedication

A cornerstone was laid February 23, 1891. The archive box of the old monument was sealed in the cornerstone of the new one. The monument was dedicated July 21, 1891, the 30th anniversary of the Battle of First Manassas (First Bull Run) where the regiment "poured out its first blood."

A parade led by W.L.I Major R.C. Gilchrist "who was mounted on a coal black charger," and composed of the W.L.I., Clinch Rifles, Sumter Guards, German Artillery and Lafayette Artillery wended its way down King Street to Broad Street before entering the park through the Meeting Street gates. In attendance were members of the Confederate Survivors Association and the Washington Light Infantry Veterans Association.

Among the dignitaries were Mayor George D. Bryan and City Council, former Mayor William A. Courtenay, Judge James Simons, the Rev. C.C. Pinckney, Brigadier General T.A. Huguenin, Colonel A.G. Magrath and Charles Inglesby, corporation counsel.

At 6 p.m. Maj. Gilchrist gave the signal and the band struck up *Dixie,* the Lafayette Artillery fired its guns and the bells of St. Michael's pealed. Twenty-five young women, 22 of whom were the relatives of past Washington Light Infantry commanders, tugged the cords of the monument's interwoven wrapping composed of a giant United States flag and an equally large South Carolina flag. As they released, halyards on the nearby flagstaff were pulled unveiling the monument with the two flags fluttering over it.

The Rev. E.C. Egerton of Aiken delivered both an opening prayer and benediction for the occasion. The keynote speaker was Judge Charles H. Simonton, president of the Washington Light Infantry Veterans Association. He spoke of Wade Hampton's oration at the unveiling of the Washington Light Infantry's first monument and provided a detailed history of the regiment.

Bibliography

Secondary Sources

Bartlett, Irving H. John C. Calhoun—A Biography. New York: W.W. Norton & Co., 1993.

Borick, Carl P. A Gallant Defense—The Siege of Charleston, 1780. Columbia: University of South Carolina Press, 2003.

Breibart, Solomon. Exploration in Charleston's Jewish History. Charleston: History Press, 2005.

Burstein, Andrew. The Passion of Andrew Jackson. New York: Alfred A. Knopf, 2003.

Burton, E. Milby. The Siege of Charleston 1861-1865. Columbia: University of South Carolina Press, 1970.

Cisco, Walter Brian. Henry Timrod—A Biography. Cranbury: Associated University Presses, 2004.

Cisco, Walter Brian. Wade Hampton: Confederate Warrior, Conservative Statesman. Washington, D.C.: Brassey's, 2004.

Coulter, E. Merton. George Walton Williams—The Life of a Southern Merchant and Banker 1820-1903. Athens: Hibriten Press, 1976.

DeGregorio, William A. The Complete Book of the U.S. Presidents. New York: Random House, 1997. (Reprint).

Detzer, David. Allegiance—Fort Sumter, Charleston and the Beginning of the Civil War. New York: Harcourt Inc., 2001.

Edgar, Walter. South Carolina: A History. Columbia: University of South Carolina Press, 1998.

Edgar, Walter. The South Carolina Encyclopedia. Columbia: University of South Carolina Press, 2006.

Fraser, Walter J. Jr. Charleston! Charleston! The History of a Southern City. Columbia: University of South Carolina Press, 1989.

Grossman, Michael. The Power of Memory: How Charleston Remembers the Holocaust. Charleston Magazine (Vol. 11 No. 4) July/August 1997: 20-26.

Heisser, David C.R. Warrior Queen of the Ocean: The Story of Charleston and Its Seal. South Carolina Historical Magazine (Vol. 93 No.1) January 1992: 167-195.

Hicks, Brian and Kropf, Schuyler. Raising the Hunley—The Remarkable History and Recovery of the Lost Confederate Submarine. New York: Ballantine Books, 2002.

Johnson, Allen (Editor). Dictionary of American Biography. New York: Charles Scribner's Sons, 1958.

Longacre, Edward G. Gentleman and Soldier: The Extraordinary Life of Gen. Wade Hampton. Nashville: Rutledge Hill Press, 2003

Phelps, W. Chris. The Bombardment of Charleston 1863-1865. Gretna: Pelican Publishing Co. Inc., 1999.

Poston, Jonathan H. The Buildings of Charleston—A Guide to the City's Architecture. Columbia: University of South Carolina Press, 1997.

Ripley, Warren. The Battery—Charleston, South Carolina. Charleston: The News and Courier and Charleston Evening Post, 1977.

Rosen, Robert N. Confederate Charleston—An Illustrated History of the City and the People During the Civil War. Columbia:

University of South Carolina Press, 1994.

Rosen, Robert N.. A Short History of Charleston. Charleston: Peninsula Press, 1994 (Second Printing).

Savas, Theodore P. and Dameron, David J. A Guide to the Battles of the American Revolution. New York: Savas Beatie LLC, 2006.

Schreadley, R.L. Valor and Virtue: The Washington Light Infantry In Peace and In War. Columbia: Reprint Company, 1997.

Seigler, Robert S. A Guide to Confederate Monuments in South Carolina—"Passing the Silent Cup." Columbia: S.C. Dept. of Archives and History, 1997

Von Kolnitz, Alfred H. A Panorama of Three Centuries of History Viewed From Charleston's Famous Battery. Charleston: Walker, Evans and Cogswell, 1937.

Wallace, David Duncan. South Carolina—A Short History 1520-1948. Chapel Hill: University of North Carolina Press, 1951.

The starting point for research in almost every case was Charleston's newspapers: the News and Courier, the Charleston Evening Post, and the Post and Courier, which are available on microfilm at the Charleston County Main Library at 68 Calhoun Street and the Charleston Library Society at 164 King Street. Aside from the microfilm, the Main Library maintains a clipping service in its vertical file.

In addition, the South Carolina Room at the Main Library has copies of the Charleston Yearbooks, City Council Journals and many other useful materials. Another great source of primary documents is Charleston's Record Management.

The following people were instrumental in providing information concerning the parks and monuments:

Charleston Holocaust Memorial
Jennifer Phillips Henriques

Century Plaques
Arthur Wilcox

George Washington Statue
J. Grahame Long, Carol Ezell-Gilson, Charles Waring III,
William Cleveland and John Michel

Charleston Parks Department
Steve Livingston, Bill Turner, Danny Burbage, Dustin Clemens

Marion Square
Sheila Wertimer, Richard J. Van Seters, Laura Solano and Peter
Stutsman

Governor Robert Gibbes Plaque
Annette Metz

Dancing Children
Marguerite Valk Gussenhoven

Nathaniel Johnson Monument
Ernestine Fellers

Waterfront Park
Stu Dawson and Varoujan Hagopian

John Christie Plaque
Dr. Todd E. Harburn

William Moultrie Monument
George Brailsford and Richard Crites

This project would not have been possible without the assistance
of the following: Family: Janet Russell, Darlene, Jennifer and Katharine Young, Tatjana and Andrei Mihailovic; Friends: Donn Pittman,
Nina Logan, Michael Brown, Al Ray, Jan Elder, Deb Harnish, James
Morrison, Brian Behr and Brandon Sheffield.